I0485913

How to Buy a Business With Little or No Money Down

By Ade Asefeso MCIPS MBA

First Edition

ISBN-13: 978-1517086626

ISBN-10:1517086620

Publisher: AA Global Sourcing Ltd
Website: http://www.aaglobalsourcing.com

1

Table of Contents

Disclaimer

This publication is designed to provide competent and reliable information regarding the subject matter covered. However, it is sold with the understanding that the author and publisher are not engaged in rendering professional advice. The authors and publishers specifically disclaim any liability that is incurred from the use or application of contents of this book.

Dedication

To my family and friends who seems to have been sent here to teach me something about who I am supposed to be. They have nurtured me, challenged me, and even opposed me…. But at every juncture has taught me!

This book is dedicated to my lovely boys, Thomas, Michael and Karl. Teaching them to manage their finance will give them the lives they deserve. They have taught me more about life, presence, and energy management than anything I have done in my life.

Chapter 1: Introduction

Some entrepreneurs would rather buy an established business than start one from scratch. The advantages include established customers, current sales and ongoing cash flow. The downside is that the current owner will want compensation for the value he has created in the business. Most owners want upfront payment for the business and then hand over the keys; however, with a little luck, you can find an owner that will work with you to buy the business with no money upfront and payments spread out over time.

Before you approach the owner of the business you want to buy, you need to do some preparation. Check your credit rating and clean up any errors on your credit report. Pay down credit so that your available credit is higher, which will improve your credit score. A high credit score shows the business owner you are financially strong and are responsible with money. Develop a resume that highlights your expertise in that type of business. If you want to buy a recruitment agency and you have no experience running a recruitment agency , it will be a challenge to show the owner you can generate enough profit to pay him.

Find a Motivated Seller.

Patience and research are key. The seller should be highly motivated to exit his company. That could mean finding a seller who has had his business on the market for 6 months to a year with no buyers. Another example would be an owner who is close to retirement and is amenable to a stream of income over several years rather than a lump sum. It could also mean a business whose owner has passed away or a partnership where one partner wants to leave.

Find an Underperforming Business.

A business that is barely profitable or even losing money is a better bet for you to buy with no money down than a highly profitable business. The trick is to have the experience and management ability to turn the business around. If the business fails, you will have lost the time investment you have made since you took over ownership.

Obtaining Owner Financing.

Owner financing of a business is similar to seller financing of a home. Instead of getting a bank loan, the owner lends you the money. The purchase contract specifies the interest rate, the principal, which is purchase price of the business, the number of payments, the amount of payment and what happens if you miss a payment. Owner financing increases the cash outlay for the business but does allow you to buy it with no money upfront.

Pay on Performance.

Pay on performance is an arrangement in which you and the owner of the business agree to performance benchmarks for the business. When those benchmarks are reached, you pay the owner an agreed upon amount. The benchmarks take place over a 1 to 5 year period and may be based on revenues, operating income or net income. The total amount of payments is capped by the agreed purchase price. The owner may prefer the benchmarks to be revenue oriented since you, as the new owner, can add additional expenses to decrease the net income. For example, you could lease a new car under the business or pay yourself a higher salary.

Chapter 2: Ways to Start a Business

There are two ways to start a business.

Build one from scratch or buy one that is already up and running. The first can be more time consuming and uncertain as you are the one who has to discover what works and what doesn't. The second, while perhaps not the best solution for 'boots trappers', offers some real advantages to the new entrepreneur willing to invest their cash or find the finance.

No business, even the previously most successful, comes with a guarantee of future success, but an existing business does offer either proven it's worth already or an opportunity for growth; given a little tender loving care (TLC). So, in an up and running traditional 'bricks and mortar' venture or an online business with an established record and infrastructure in place, at least removes some element of risk.

An existing business also has a history you can use to look back on what has worked before and perhaps more importantly, what hasn't. This allows you to continue to replicate the profitable, and to discard the rest. In fact, the very reason you may be interested in a business in the first place is because you can see past mistakes and have a plan for putting them right.

You can also use the history of a business to forecast what is likely to happen in the future. For instance, looking through a company's accounts will give you a good idea of probable future running costs, something you would never really know beforehand when growing a new business from the roots up.

Get results sooner.

Stepping into an existing business also gives you a little more confidence than with a startup, since you will be able to draw on the knowledge and experience of existing staff, all of which should help make your learning curve less steep and with staff, equipment, systems and hopefully customers, already in place, with you should be doing business faster than is possible with a startup.

What is more, you will also have an established presence in the marketplace so customers and clients are aware of you and what you have to offer, achieving the same with a new business takes time and certainly effort.

While you will want to revisit some areas of an existing business and put your personal stamp on them, you will have a framework from which to develop, so you won't have to focus on every part of the business at once as you do with a startup, giving you more time to concentrate on areas that generate sales and add value for your customers.

Of course, buying an existing business is a financial commitment, and even though one of the advantages of buying a going concern is that you may have been able to acquire the assets at a knockdown price, you will still want to limit your risk and financial exposure as much as possible.

Try the online option.

In the 'old days' not so long ago! this wouldn't have been an option, but for anyone thinking of becoming an entrepreneur, going online is a very cost-effective alternative to the traditional 'bricks and mortar' business.

Even if you are buying a 'bricks and mortar' business, you will almost certainly need to have an online presence where information can be found about you and your business and customers can purchase from an ecommerce shop.

Being online also offers great opportunities to promote your existing products and services along multiple channels, as well as enabling geographically distant consumers and those who prefer to 'computer shop' to buy from you. These days, having an online presence also means that every business potentially has a global audience.

The type of business you go for will dictate, of course, the level of investment required and your day-to-day involvement in it. So here, are four things you may wish to consider before choosing one sort over another.

1. With online businesses you won't have to invest in expensive equipment, premises or staff at least not until you are really successful. That is not to say you

can't spend big if you want to; high profile, established domains go for many millions but you can start for much, much, less.

2. You will get faster income generation from an online business since it should already be attracting internet traffic and converting it into paying customers and clients. Those are real enough numbers that you can count.

3. Scalability also means that you can develop an online business much more quickly than the traditional kind. You can do this either by concentrating on adding value to the original business, or replicating the same model in other market niches. So, even a little way down the line, you will have something of real value.

4. By buying an existing online business, you may not have to invest the same commitment in time that you would have to with a traditional business. The nature of the online world means that once a business is set up, it takes much less effort to keep the machine 'well oiled' and working.

Of course, before buying any business you should always undertake the necessary due diligence to investigate any claims made by the vendor using appropriate legal and financial professionals to advise you as necessary.

Then, if what they tell you feels right, follow your instincts and get started in business; it's the only way to build a rewarding and fulfilling future for yourself and ensure that you stay in control of your life at the same time.

But whether it's a real world or virtual business you are buying, make sure you continue to keep learning all you can about online marketing and social media skills because what is required to achieve success is continually changing.

Chapter 3: How to Start a Business With No Money

"I have got a great idea for a business. But I don't have any money to start it up."

The above phrase is something I have heard again and again and again from young poeple, friends, and sometimes even colleagues. While it's true that a generous credit line, a team of investors, or an uncle with deep pockets can make starting a company easier, not having money is no excuse. If you are confident that you have a product or service people want, don't allow the lack of capital to deter you from your business goals. By pivoting, grinding it out, getting creative, and differentiating yourself, you can bootstrap your way to a successful business.

1. Pivot. Use services to generate cash flow and fund a product-based business.

Starting a service-oriented business is easy: First, you provide services, and then you collect funds. But a product-based business often requires significant up-front capital to get it up and running. If you are in this situation, consider selling services to generate cash flow and to build up funds for a product-based business.

2. Grind it out. There is no substitute for sweat equity.

Sometimes you have to get into the trenches and make it happen. During the first 3 years of business at my company, AA Global Sourcing Ltd, I knocked on doors, worked my own booth, and closed my own deals. I set up a table at the local college's business school, hired five college students to work solely on commission, and knocked on people's doors 7-8 hours per day looking for business. For those 3 years I didn't receive a salary. But I believed in my service, and I believed we could be successful and the hard work eventually paid off.

3. Get creative. Funding sources are everywhere.

Traditional entrepreneurship philosophy dictates that, to be successful, you should stick with one thing and not deviate from it. But desperate times call for desperate measures. If you are having trouble finding access to funds, there are a number of creative things you can do.

a. Get a credit line. It is not uncommon for most startup businesses to rely on a line of credit. The American Express Plum Card, for example, offers a 60-day term for payment rather than a typical 30-day term. Some banks or credit institutions offer credit designed to allow growth in the early stages of business. A word of caution: to keep from getting bogged down in debt when you are trying to expand a business, keep purchases to a minimum.

b. Use an Incubator. If you believe you have a solid idea and a workable business plan, you may want to consider a business incubator. Upon acceptance, these programs provide funding designed specifically to financially assist a startup company. Sometimes they offer office space or shared administrative services. Most incubation programs are sponsored by local or regional economic development organizations, and some are sponsored by colleges and universities.

c. Find an Accelerator. These are much like incubators in that they are designed to provide funding; however, an accelerator expects a rapid response to its investment. If you are prepared and ready to hit the market quickly, this is a great option.

d. Crowdfund. Crowdfunding platforms are changing the face of capital, whether you are growing a tech business, filming a movie, or selling jewellery. Kickstarter and other crowdfunding platforms allow the public to invest a small percentage of money in return for a future buy-in.

4. Differentiate yourself. Small things make a big difference.

Once you get to a million dollars in revenue, your odds of funding increase exponentially. Banks, for example, look at funding strictly from this perspective. Banks don't care what kind of company you are they simply look at your profit/loss statement and make a decision. If you are a profitable company with a million in revenue and good personal credit score, there is a good chance that a bank will lend you up to $200,000.

If you have some revenue coming in but need an extra boost to get to the million-dollar mark, make sure to consider every possible way that your company can differentiate itself. Do you have a letter of commitment from a notable investor? Do you have some revenue or a contract to get some revenue? Do you have valuable intellectual property with the potential to generate revenue? Differentiators like these can make the difference between getting funded and being overlooked by investors and lenders.

The only real way to start generating revenue for your business is to roll up your sleeves and get to work. Despite what others may tell you, there is no easy shortcut to profit. But if you are confident you have a product or service that people want, you can propel your way to the top by pivoting, grinding it out, getting creative, and differentiating yourself.

Chapter 4: Buying Under Performing Businesses.

The fundamental principle of investing is to buy low and sell high. Every investor seeks to achieve this principle, regardless of what they invest in. Whether you trade stocks, bonds, gold or real estate, everyone seeks to find the diamond in the ruff or "The Bargain". You should look at business ownership as an investment, and just like all the other investments, there are "Bargains" here as well and you could make a fortune buying under-performing businesses as long as you know what to look for.

My definition of a business that is under-performing is a business that is not reaching its full potential. It has been a long practice of Asset Management companies to seek out businesses in a specific industry that are under performing, fix them, hold them for several years and then sell them for a profit. Now Asset Management companies typically have access to millions of dollars and seek large companies, however you don't need to have millions, to duplicate the same process. You can seek smaller companies which are readily available and require a lot less money to buy, thus for $100K you could own 3-4 small businesses and keep growing from there. The key to finding an under-performing business is to know what to look for, ask the right questions, do some investigative work and come up with a business plan and strategy on how to fix the problems that maybe facing that particular business. Here are some of the things to look for.

1. Owners Participation

Owner's participation is key to any business success and most absentee owners leave too much responsibility to key employees who have nothing at stake to make a business more successful. These businesses typically have higher than usual costs, lack in customer service, and have ineffective or non-existent marketing campaign. These are all easily fixed with an active owner and if you must have a manager running your business, give your manager an incentive to be more diligent. Profit sharing, bonus program or compensation based on performance are all excellent ways of motivating your staff. There are plenty of businesses where the owner is actively participating in the daily operations of the business, but lack the "business experience" of running the business. Most successful businesses have an owner who is the CEO and the CFO of their company and are actually working ON the business, not IN the business. Here are some examples of this.

A plumber who does his own work does not have time to actively network the business, restaurant owner who works in the kitchen, instead of managing the restaurant. When the owner is too busy working IN the business, that business will typically have the same problems as if it was being run absentee.

2. Distressed Owner.

A Distressed owner is someone who is selling because they are retiring, getting a divorce, relocating or illness. Most of the time their companies and businesses are doing very well, but they are selling below market value for a fast sale. Keep in mind that you still must do a thorough due diligence, to verify the reason for the sale.

As you do your due diligence, the important things to look for, besides all the things I have mentioned above, are sales trends over a period of 3 years if possible. If there is a trend down ward year after year, ask why, it's a good sign of mismanagement, but could be a sign of something worse, like a product getting obsolete, contracts being lost, etc. Stay away from businesses that sell trendy products, since trends get hot and cold. Interview the owner and find out why sales have been going down. Talk to employees if possible, landlords, suppliers, etc. The important thing for you to identify is what can be done to improve the company and the business and then ask yourself if it is something you can accomplish. If the answer is yes, then you got yourself a "Bargain", if the answer is no, move on.

Here is one more thing to consider. Some of the best bargains are in Franchise Resale's and they might be the easiest to do your due diligence. One of the best tools available to anyone looking to buy a Franchise is the ability to speak to existing Franchisees, Area Developers, and Regional Managers. These people could be a great source of information for you and may give you an outline of what needs to be done in order to make a business work. This is only available in the Franchise Industry, so if you are a new business buyer, or even a seasoned one, look at Franchises first.

Chapter 5: Can You Buy a Business With No Money Down?

Yes, you can. It's not easy, but it can be done.

As a general rule, buying a pre-existing business can be a very good idea, but as with everything else in this economy, to make sure it will be a successful venture, you have to proceed with caution, do your due diligence, and understand the pros and cons.

We all know the principle of leverage.

In its primary application it is where you use tools and positioning to increase your power and ability to lift or work with heavy objects.

Archimedes stated "Give me a lever long enough and I can move the world".

Well, we don't need to move the world and we are not talking about moving heavy objects but in its truest application, leverage can be used in financial transactions just as in mechanical applications.

You can use the principles of financial leverage to buy a good, solid business without using your own money.

Financial leverage is a fancy way of saying "Other People's Money".

When you use other people's money to buy a business it's called a leveraged buyout or LBO.

Leveraged transactions (LBOs) work this way:

The buyer finances the transaction with funds borrowed against the assets and projected cash flows of the business being acquired. Through the use of proven deal structure the buyer accommodates the needs of the business owner yet creates a means to defer additional cash required to purchase the business from them.

Leveraged buyouts are financed chiefly with borrowed capital (from lenders and even from the business seller themselves), not only because such funds are readily available, but also because if you used cash to buy equity you actually lower the return on your investment than when transactions are financed predominately with debt and cash deferral deal structure.

Debt is less costly than equity financing for two reasons. First, equity is at greater risk. It is subordinated to debt, trade creditors, and others as to rights to the cash flow of the business.

If you funded the acquisition through bringing in equity investors, they expect substantially higher returns on their investment than do lenders.

Second, interest on debt is a deductible expense whereas dividends on equity are paid with after-tax profit. So from a buyer's standpoint it is more costly for your business to provide a return on equity than it is to provide the same level of return on debt.

You structure the leveraged buyout of a business by using the assets and cash flow of the business to finance and pay for the entire purchase price; both the cash down payment and the monthly instalments to pay for the business.

The business buys itself and you own it.

This way of buying business has been going on for decades; earliest actual reports of LBOs date back to World War II and no doubt occurred even further back than that.

In fact leveraged transactions such as LBOs are so accepted by the financial communities that an entire financial services industry supports these types of transactions.

Even the Business Brokerage industry is trying to educate people to the benefit of using creative ways to structure deals.

Brokers understand that the more they can educate buyers to use the same tools as we discuss in this book, the more businesses they can sell.

We know that if you are reading this, that you might be interested in buying a business of your own. But you probably have two main questions.

1. Who would sell me a good business if I don't put my own money into it?

And ...

2. Can I really do it?

Those are good questions; we will answer them directly.

Right now we are entering a period of tremendous availability of good solid businesses; baby boomers that own businesses get older every day and many of them need to find a way to exit their business as best they can. Remember just because you do not put cash of your own into the transaction; it does not mean that the seller does not get a cash down-payment and other acceptable terms to satisfy them in order for them to sell their business to you.

Yes. Leveraged buyouts and buying businesses without using your own money is done every day countless times in the United States and Europe.

Most people think that they have to have a lot of their own money to buy a business.

That is just not true.

It does take money to buy a business but again we are talking about learning how to use other people's money in this chapter; not your own!

Perhaps you have another question like "I have heard that it is very hard to find money to start a business; why would someone provide money for me to buy a business?"

Here is why.

1. It is cheaper smarter safer and much faster to buy a good business rather than to start one.

2. Established businesses have proven revenues and cash flow.

3. They have existing customers and supplier relationships.

4. The financial communities know that it is much safer for them to put money into an established business as compared to a startup business.

5. The financial community that we mention above is familiar and comfortable in working with business people in leveraged transactions for solid established businesses.

They understand their business and what is more they are comfortable and understand the businesses of their clients.

They know that asset-based transactions are a good investment for them and that historically they have worked well for many buyers who use their services (and capital) to buy businesses.

Keep in mind, as an example, if you buy a successful business for $1 million using other people's money; you own a significant asset that produces a regular income.

It doesn't matter if you bought the business without using any of your own money.

When the financing is paid off you will own a $1 million business asset free and clear. Paid for by other people's money that is paid back from the cash flow of the business!

The business market favours the knowledgeable buyer!

Right now we are entering a period of tremendous availability of good solid businesses as baby boomer business owners look to exit their businesses.

Here is a couple of interesting statistics from the business brokerage industry:

Over 90 percent of the people who began the search to buy business fail to complete a purchase and they look at business for sale listings for eighteen months yet still never buy.

Only 25 percent of business broker listings sell; 75 percent of the business listings do not sell.

So we have a very significant and dynamic event shaping up. More business owners than ever in history are reaching a point where they need to sell, faced with people who want to buy but 90% of the time, never do!

Why do "buyers" not buy and "sellers" not sell?

I have been involved in literally hundreds of types of transactions over the course of my business career and I can answer this question with absolute certainty.

Lack of knowledge.

Buyers that do not know how to find, evaluate, structure and negotiate transactions and business owners who do not understand how proper valuation and deal structure can help them sell their business for a fair (in some cases premium) value and with a structure that optimizes tax benefits for them.

For buyers that understand these things there will be hundreds of thousands if not millions of dollars made by them over the next few years as they are presented with opportunities from thousands of business owners motivated to sell their business.

Again you don't need your own capital, you just need to learn how manageable leveraged transactions are done and go out and do it.

You have probably seen the big business buyers always in the news. There are hundreds, if not thousands, of smaller business buyer success stories that happen every day that you never hear about; setting their life up so that when they retire, it will be with a pile of money and all they are doing is buying businesses using other people's money.

The huge number of available businesses out there and business owners interested to sell their business coupled with the fact that there are not enough knowledgeable, truly knowledgeable buyers out there is one of the main reasons why this works when you become one of those knowledgeable buyers.

The point that we make in this book is that the cash for the down-payment does not have to be yours.

1. Asset based and collateralized lending has been around for hundreds and thousands of years.

2. Using the assets and cash flow of a business to help you buy it is something that is commonly accepted in the financial community.

3. There is a whole industry of lenders and investors who focus just on that very thing.

4. There are literally hundreds and thousands of investors and lenders that put money into businesses based on the assets of the business and its cash flow and ability to pay the money back.

All of the above, are the reasons that leveraged transactions have worked in the past, they work today and will work in the future.

Chapter 6: Creative Financing for Buyers with Limited Capital

Today's economic downturn has created great buying opportunities for those interested in acquiring a business. Like all investments, the goal is to buy-low and sell-high. For those willing to take the risk, creative financing tactics are becoming more common. Here are a number of options for individuals or businesses looking for additional financing above their down payment.

1. Seller Financing: Increasingly, buyers and lenders are looking to the seller for financing as they try to put a transaction together. In such a scenario, the seller will hold a note at an agreed upon interest rate for a specific term or amortization; generally ranging from 3 to 10 years.

The terms of the sale may include a balloon payment three to five years after the purchase date. It is a way of giving the buyer time to get up and running and to establish a successful track record with the business.

Seller financing makes the bank more comfortable with the transaction. Lenders know they have a seller who has a vested interest in the success of the business rather than one who will take their money and run. Most lenders are requiring a portion of seller financing in the transaction.

2. Small Business Administration (SBA) Loans:
In sales of a business, conventional loans usually aren't available, so a buyer may want to consider going to a Small Business Administration lender, which has a number of loan options.

The SBA guarantees a portion of the loan. The buyer pays an SBA loan fee that allows them to get funding for a loan the bank couldn't do conventionally. If an SBA guaranteed loan goes into default, the SBA will pay the lending institution a percentage of any deficit left after liquidating the collateral.

3. Earnouts: Earnout financing involves a certain dollar amount agreed on by the buyer and seller to be paid to the seller based on the performance of the company after the transaction is completed.

Earnouts can be structured in a variety of ways and can be based on different financial benchmarks such as a company's revenues or gross profits.

Earnout financing is often used for companies that are in a turnaround situation or when buyers are purchasing on potential, rather than on historical cash flow. It is also a great way to bridge the gap during negotiations when both parties are slightly off on the amount willing to pay or willing to accept to complete a transaction.

4. Mezzanine Financing: In mergers and acquisitions, mezzanine financing is another alternative for a buyer looking for capital where the financing package may include interest rates as high as 20 to 30 percent.

The lenders in this situation are typically high net worth individuals who are expecting a larger return on their investment. They are lending in a junior lien or a position behind the bank and seller financing. The loans are typically made with limited sources of collateral, thus the request for higher interest rates. This financing is often used in funding goodwill or reputation in an acquisition.

Typical Funding Scenario - In a million dollar transaction, the buyer would be expected to have a 20 percent down payment, sometimes more depending on the industry. The seller may hold an additional 10 to 20 percent in seller financing, and the lending institution would offer a combination of conventional or SBA financing to cover the difference, depending on collateral available.

A buyer and the lending institution must evaluate a company's cash flow and determine if it is adequate to cover their debt service and provide a reasonable return on their investment. Lending institutions will also be examining whether a buyer's coverage ratio, or excess cash flow after all debt is paid, is adequate to cover their needs.

Talk with a business intermediary representing the company you are considering purchasing. They will know if the owner is willing to consider seller financing, earnouts or other creative financing ideas. Based on your available capital, the business intermediary should be able to tell you whether you will be considered for the purchase and may also provide you references to various lenders that are familiar with financing the purchase of a business.

We will look into all of the above creative financing in the later chapters of this book.

Chapter 7: Mezzanine Financing

Nothing is as simple as it first seems; that applies to many pieces of the great jigsaw puzzle that makes up the financial world, and equity and debt are no exceptions.

They are at opposite ends of the spectrum, and in between lies an entire world where ingenious financiers and lawyers have developed all sorts of techniques for making equity more debt-like, and debt more equity-like.

The technical term for much of this is not "magic," but rather mezzanine investing.

Mezzanine falls squarely into that space between equity and debt, and has elements of both investment banking and private equity and it might just be better than either.

What is Mezzanine?

In a typical leveraged buyout, the private equity firm contributes its own equity (the cash it has on hand) and then raises debt from banks to cover the rest of the purchase price.

It's just like buying a house; you front whatever cash you can for the down payment, and then take out a mortgage to cover the rest of the price.

With houses it's fairly simple and (most) people only have one mortgage, but when you are buying entire companies, often you need multiple different types of debt, with each one coming from a different investor.

Mezzanine is "in between" debt and equity in such a deal; mezzanine investors take on more risk than the normal debt providers, have a lower claim to the company's assets, and expect a higher return.

"Mezzanine" itself is usually a more "junior" form of debt that can sometimes be converted to equity; sometimes private equity firms themselves provide the debt and other times it comes from banks, but dedicated mezzanine funds provide the bulk of the loans.

I could go on about what mezzanine is and what it isn't, but a friend of mine recently had the chance to interview a Partner at a dedicated mezzanine fund; so you will get to hear all about it directly from the source.

Question: So, tell me about your journey. How did you end up in mezzanine?

Answer: I went to a good US school; not Ivy League, but still a good reputation and then joined a US-based investment bank as an analyst in the Merger and Acquisition Department.

I stayed on until I was promoted to associate, and as things were starting to slow down (in the last recession), I decided it might be a good time to do an

MBA, so I went to Europe for that; I was in my mid-to-late twenties back then.

At the time my intentions were to get into private equity; a lot of people go into mezz because they want to do private equity and become a Principal there. If you do normal debt deals you feel very much like a lender, but mezzanine, with its fund structure, is much more like being an investor.

So there I was, looking at private equity and researching it over the course of my MBA when I began to look more closely at mezzanine as another option. With mezz, you do largely the same work as private equity, but you do deals with a much greater "frequency" as there Is considerably less portfolio management at least when things are working as they should be.

It's sort of like "private equity lite," which was a great fit for me as a former banker I didn't have much operational experience and I didn't want to be as involved operationally as you might be in private equity. But it's also not as impersonal or mechanical as being a senior lender, since you look at qualitative criteria as well.

They focused on deals, which appealed to me. I saw it as a way to become an investor while still ensuring that I could keep working on deals as much as I had in banking.

In mezz, you also piggy-back on the efforts of the private equity guys quite a lot; you might sit as an observer on the Board, but as an observer you wouldn't be taking an owner's direct decisions.

This is a pretty standard state of affairs unless the company gets into a restructuring, at which point you may end up in an equity-holding situation. Otherwise, you get pretty much the same information a lender would get; monthly reports on points such as management accounts.

Question: Do you still find yourself wanting to do private equity?

Answer: Actually I came to like mezz a lot; it's much more diverse, not just in terms of volume of deals, but also in terms of sectors, geographies, deal sizes, and so on, whereas you tend to specialize in private equity. I don't think that would work for me now.

Question: What are the typical entry points into the field?

Answer: The standard path is to join as a post-MBA associate following prior experience at an investment bank in a team such as Leveraged Finance or Merger and Acquisition.

Some people enter after working for a year or two as analysts at investment banks; this is low-risk for the employer since it's inexpensive and it's not such a big deal to train them.

But they don't want someone straight out of university; however two years in banking candidates gain confidence with modelling, valuation and how the practice of a buyout works.

So Merger and Acquisition, Leveraged Finance or Corporate Finance are all good, but someone from, say, Equity Research, would be less suitable; their models aren't as deep, and we want people with deal experience, partially for the obvious reasons, but also because they will know the realities of a work style that involves peaks and troughs.

For the post-MBA associate, we look for more or less the same qualities; ideally someone who was an analyst at a private equity firm or mezz house, or perhaps in distressed debt.

We are not so interested in consultants with MBAs; they work better in mainstream private equity where the operational skill-set is more important; we want modellers more than PowerPoint jockeys.

But across the board there seem to be fewer consultants than bankers in private equity, with the exception of the German-speaking world. Typically we see more interest from people with Merger and Acquisition and Leveraged Finance backgrounds anyway.

A Day in the Life of a Mezzanine Investor.

Question: Speaking of peaks and troughs, what are the hours like? What is the typical rhythm?

Answer: The work is deal-based, so you can have flat periods but then you could have two big deals come along at the same time.

On top of that, there is monitoring the portfolio, which is generally steady and quite light work, but if something blows up then that is a huge spike in working hours.

So it's not investment banking; not as extreme as Merger and Acquisition but it's more than your typical 9-to-5. So perhaps 9-to-7 in calmer times, all the way up to the full all-nighter when deals heat up.

Question: So what is the day-to-day nature of the work? How do you raise funds and source deals?

Answer: As with any fund-based business, everything starts with raising money from investors. This is largely the same as private equity; you put together the materials and go out to meet Limited Partners.

An analyst might get involved with putting together the Private Placement Memorandum and presentations, and the more senior staff will be on the road meeting with potential investors.

Once you raise the funds, the next step is sourcing deals, which is primarily a matter of leveraging relationships with private equity firms and senior lenders.

You want to be their first call for mezzanine financing, so that involves a lot of networking;

networking is important across everything in Leveraged Finance, but for LBO-mezz "networking" consists of meeting with sponsors and lenders, and less so with Merger and Acquisition advisors and the contacts that first bring in the deals.

Question: So now you have the funding and the deals; what is next? What exactly do you do on a deal, and how is it different from normal private equity?

Answer: Once the deals come in, you need to do the analysis.

It's the same sort of analysis that you did expect at a private equity sponsor, but with the advantage of being somewhat pre-packaged.

"Pre-packaged" just means that when the opportunity comes to you, other parties such as the consultants, bankers, accountants, and lawyers have already done serious due diligence work.

So you get to piggy-back on their work and save a lot of time, which results in lower expenses; but that can also mean lower management fees paid to mezz funds.

The analysis still involves a lot of financial modelling; we need to do plenty of sensitivity analyses to work out how much of a 'blanket' we'll have in different scenarios; financial, operational, macroeconomic, and so on.

Naturally this affects how we structure deals and of course when structuring such a deal, we often need to negotiate with the other parties, although occasionally we do this on a 'take-it-or-leave-it' basis. The legal points are then sorted out once we agree on all the commercial elements.

Question: Okay, so essentially if you like modelling and analytical work but you don't like due diligence or the operational side, mezzanine is a great fit for you.

What about once the deal closes? How much portfolio monitoring do you do?

Answer: This part is relatively smooth unless there is a problem; we might review the monthly management accounts, meet with the executives at least once a year, and go to quarterly Board meetings.

When there is a problem such as a covenant breach or the need to refinance (whether as a restructuring or simply as part of an acquisition by the portfolio company) then we put in a great deal more effort.

We will need to revise and update the model, negotiate with all the stakeholders, and if things get ugly, also negotiate terms with the Restructuring advisors or the buyers of distressed assets.

In the later case, when people start taking haircuts or when sponsors walk away we are not automatically in the sponsors' role as the next-in-line; sometimes a distressed investor will step in to fulfil that role.

So you hope that you don't end up in these situations, but you need to protect yourself and be prepared for the possibility via appropriate attention to the deal structure and the legal side.

Question: What sort of person tends to thrive in mezzanine investing? Is it just what we discussed before; someone who enjoys modelling but isn't as interested in the operational side?

Answer: It is similar to what is required to do well in private equity; it is less high-profile, though, so you need to be sure that you are happy with that.

The work itself can be similar, though, so you need to like being close to the action and not just sitting in an office.

It is social since you spend a lot of time out in the field, but you also need to like the analysis and doing the analysis in a flexible way that lets you look at different scenarios.

That is a consequence of the greater variety in investment types, meaning that the process is less formulaic. It sometimes appeals to bankers who want a more entrepreneurial environment than what they did get working at a bank; similar to what you might see in other fund-based businesses.

Question: How are mezzanine firms structured and how much do you get paid?

Answer: Very direct, I like your style!

The structure is similar to a private equity firm, so you will see positions for Analyst, Associate, Director and Partner, possibly with some ranks in between.

In my organization the ranks are a little blurry in terms of responsibilities, but generally an analyst won't get carry, and associates may or may not depending on the firm.

If you don't get carry, you need to make sure you are on Partner-track (and if you are a post-MBA associate, you definitely need to be on Partner-track) this isn't banking where we have outsized bonuses, so the main reward comes from the carry.

The base salaries range from around £60k ($100K USD) for analysts up through £100k ($165K USD) for the Partners, and the bonuses might range from 30% to 100% of those base salaries.

But the real upside is in the carry, which can be significantly more than your normal bonus depending on the firm's performance.

In short, base salaries are roughly the same as in private equity but lower management fees mean that bonuses aren't quite what you did receive at a standard private equity firm; of course, that is balanced by the fact that the hours are often better and that you spend most of your time working on real deals.

Regions, Exit Opportunities, and the Future.

Question: How does mezzanine investing differ in other regions? We are both based in the UK, but I am assuming mezzanine differs elsewhere?

Answer: In the US and at some European mid-market funds, you will see more regional specificity; these more focused firms sometimes act more like conventional private equity firms in their focus and with their increased involvement with portfolio companies.

There are some global firms in the middle market too, and some firms specialize in sponsor-less mezz, but increasingly across many firms in the wider buyout world there is a widening of focus by the big players to embrace asset strategies beyond private equity, which include mezzanine as well as various credit funds.

Question: What are the exit opportunities in the field?

Answer: People tend to stay rather than "exiting."

Some people are leaving now as they are being forced out or because things are looking less attractive, but when the industry is doing well you tend to stay on the escalator.

It's rare for people to move back to banks; they tend to come in and stay in, and if they do well they will go off on their own and raise their own fund.

Occasionally people will go into funds of funds or private equity, but that is quite rare; usually it's the other way round, and quite a few private equity analysts and associates move into mezzanine each year.

Question: Any last words of advice to readers of this book considering mezzanine?

Answer: Be sure that you are in a fund that has a good track record and that the market and specific fund dynamics will enable them to raise their next fund.

It is a fund-based business and if there is no money you can't invest, so be certain that your firm as in private equity can get through both tranquil and turbulent times.

Question: Great – thanks very much, it was really helpful to chat with you.

Answer: No problem – I will see you soon!

Mezzanine debt gets its name because it blurs the lines between what constitutes debt and equity. It is the highest-risk form of debt, but it offers some of the highest returns; a typical rate is in the range of 12% - 20% per year.

A mezzanine lender is generally brought into a buyout to displace some of the capital that would usually be invested by an equity investor.

Chapter 8: Eight Musts to Start Your Business With Little to No Capital

Entrepreneurs will often have amazing business ideas, but they put them on hold due to a lack of capital. They assume that their idea will never get far off the ground unless they have major funding behind them.

It seems that every day there is a new startup receiving millions of dollars from venture capital firms, but what you don't hear about is the several startup failures that burn through millions of dollars only to fizzle out and shut their doors forever.

If your idea and plan of execution are not well thought out from the beginning, no amount of money can turn it into a winner. Have a great idea but very little money? Don't let that stop you! Yes, there will be ridiculously long days with little to no sleep. Yes, you are going to be stressed. But those that want it bad enough will make it.

Here are 8 tips that can help you get your idea off the ground with limited funds.

1. Build your business around what you know. Instead of venturing off into uncharted territory, make sure that you build your business around your skills and knowledge. The less you have to rely on outside sources the better. When your business is built around your own personal expertise you can eliminate consultants and outside assistance.

Also, having that knowledge is sometimes all that is needed to successfully take the plunge into entrepreneurship.

2. Tell everyone you know what you are doing. Inform your family, friends, business contacts and past colleagues about your new business. Call, send emails and make your new venture known on your social-media profiles. Your friends and family members can help you spread the word, and past business contacts can introduce your brand to their professional contacts as well. This type of grassroots marketing can help introduce your company to a much larger audience.

3. Avoid unnecessary expenses. You are going to have plenty of expenses, and there are some that just can't be avoided. What you can avoid though is overspending. Take something as simple as business cards. You could drop $1,000 on 500 metal business cards that give off the "cool" factor, or you could spend $10 on 500 traditional business cards. Being frugal in the beginning can be the difference between success and a failed business.

4. Don't get buried in credit card debt. There is a smart way and a suicidal way to use credit when starting a business. New computers, office furniture, phones and supplies can all quickly add up. Instead of purchasing everything at once and throwing it all on a credit card, use your company's revenue to finance your expenses. Eliminating the stress and burden of debt will greatly increase the chances of creating a successful business.

5. Make sure your receivables policy won't sink you. If your business is a retail operation then this isn't going to apply, but if you are providing services such as consulting or products to retailers you need to make sure that your payment policy is well thought out. Can you remain above water with net-30 or net-60 terms? Don't base your receivables on what you think your customers will want. Base them on what is going to make your business operate successfully.

6. Build up sweat equity. When I first started my business I worked around the clock, handling every aspect of the business as well as the marketing and growth. All of the hard work and long days that you put in isn't for nothing. You are building a brand and your hard work is essentially increasing the value of your business. Your sweat equity will come into play if you ever decide to sell off a piece of your company or take on a partner.

7. Take advantage of free advertising and marketing. There are several ways to generate a buzz for your business without breaking the bank. Social media is a great way to gain exposure and interact with potential customers. You can also reach out to local media and offer your expertise.

Make as many local media contacts as you can and be extremely responsive with their requests. This can lead to them branding you as the local authority, generating plenty of free press for your business.

8. Get ready to hustle. Hard work is an absolute necessity, but when you are starting a business with little to no capital then you must be prepared to dedicate everything you have into making the business a success. This might mean cold calling, handling customer support, dealing with billing and accounting, and every other working part of your business. You will wear many hats and it will require the majority of your time and energy if you are to make it.

Don't let limited capital prevent you from taking a great idea and running with it. Will it be difficult and will you have some stressful situations? Of course, but that is part of entrepreneurship.

Chapter 9: Buying Business With Zero Money Down

Most sophisticated and experienced business buyers and investors (and I have talked, worked and dealt with hundreds) are good people; professionals that have learned through experience and don't mind talking about it and sharing their knowledge.

The thing is, most people don't know someone like that, and if they don't know them; how can they ask them about buying businesses and the best way to do it if you have a limited amount of capital?

There are a lot of good books out there on buying a business. They are a great resource for those people who have a lot of cash on hand to buy a business.

They are also great reference materials for those out there that want to buy a business but may not have the money to do it. But frankly it is not going to be much help to them since they do not have the money to buy a business the way that most people think is the only way to buy a business. But there are other ways and you can buy a good business without using your own money for the down-payment. This has been proven for decades time and time again.

Most people think that they have to have a lot of their own money to buy a business.

That is just not true.

It does take money to buy a business but again we are talking about learning how to use other people's money; not your own!

Perhaps you have another question like "I've heard that it is very hard to find money to start a business; why would someone provide money for me to buy a business?"

Here is why:

1. It is cheaper smarter safer and much faster to buy a good business rather than to start one.

2. Established businesses have proven revenues and cash flow.

3. They have existing customers and supplier relationships.

4. The financial communities know that it is much safer for them to put money into an established business as compared to a startup business.

The financial community that we mentioned in this chapter is familiar and comfortable in working with business people in leveraged transactions for solid established businesses.

They understand their business and what is more they are comfortable and understand the businesses of their clients. They know that asset-based transactions are a good investment for them and that historically they have worked well for many buyers who use their services (and capital) to buy businesses.

Keep in mind, as an example, if you buy a successful business for $1 million using other people's money; you own a significant asset that produces a regular income. It doesn't matter if you bought the business without using any of your own money. When the financing is paid off you will own a $1 million business asset free and clear.

Paid for by other people's money that is paid back from the cash flow of the business!

Remember that business market favours the knowledgeable buyer!

Chapter 10: Owner Finance.

This is the best way to buy a business today.

Owner financing; if you can get it, is one of the best ways to borrow money to buy a business, especially with how difficult it has become to get a startup loan from a bank.

Face it; banks are not lending to those seeking to purchase a business and, to even get them to look at your deal, you better have two or three times the collateral in relation to the potential loan amount (regardless if the business is extremely profitable or not) and just because they might look at your business loan request does not mean they will approve it. Even non-bank lenders are not lending for the purchase of a business unless it comes with a huge amount of real estate and then they will only fund based on a small loan-to-value of that real estate.

That leaves two options for most people wanting to buy the business of their dreams:

1. Friends and Family (What some call Friends, Family or Fools). Unless you have a very rich uncle, most of your friends and family are also facing financing restraints and either will not or cannot help you make a big purchase like buying a business.

2. Owner financing. Where the current owner of the business is willing to sell it to you on terms (meaning they; not the bank hold the note).

This is what we will discuss here, as this might really be the only way left to purchase a business today.

Owner financing can benefit the purchaser (you) in several ways.

1. Allows the purchaser to acquire a business without significant capital.

2. Allows the purchaser to pay off the acquisition out of the profits of the business.

3. Allows the purchaser to take ownership immediately and begin growing the business.

4. Easier to qualify for as you don't have to jump through all the hoops that banks or lenders will make you jump through like cash flow analysis, property appraisals, debt-to-income ratios, personal financial statements, etc.

5. Better terms than most banks will offer; thus, saving the new owner (the purchaser) both time and money not to mention less in regards to reporting (ongoing financial statements and tax returns) and fewer covenants.

3. More than just financing, since the current owner still has a stake in the business's success, they will provide invaluable guidance and advice well into the future.

Plus, if the current business owner believes in the business (and you can get them to believe in you) this should be a no brainer for the owner. If they hesitate without giving a very good reason, that might be a red flag to you as it might show that the current owner does not believe in the long-term viability of the business (they know something is wrong or in decline).

Benefits of Owner finance on the sell side.

1. The owner can ensure the deal doesn't fall over due to limited financing options.

2. The purchaser may be willing to pay a slightly higher price in order to secure owner finance terms.

3. The owner will earn interest on the balance of the loan.

4. The owner can hand-over the business today, while still getting paid the profits from the business for the duration of the loan.

5. As the European and American population are ageing and more businesses go on the market for sale, 'owner financing' is becoming an increasingly popular method for buying and selling businesses.

Let's look at couple of examples to show how owner financing works.

Let's say you find a business for sale, a business that you know you will have the necessary passion to work hard at and grow beyond where it stands today. The price of the business is $100,000, yet, you tried to get bank loan and even a non-bank loan and have heard nothing but "NO."

Here is where you approach the current business owner and entice them to sell you the business while carrying the note.

How your deal should work.

You tell the current owner that you will provide some down payment (this is to show good faith as well as provide a little cash incentive to the current owner). This down payment should be around 10% but could be less depending on how much you can raise. But, raising $10,000 is much easier than raising $100,000. Plus, any bank or non-bank lender would require you put up more than 10%, so 10% is really a win for you.

Now, if you put 10% down, that means the current owner would have to finance the remaining 90% or $90,000.

Here is how to approach that.

State that you will pay both principal and a comparable market interest rate (let's say for this example — 10% APR) amortized over seven years (choose a term that makes the payments work for you as well as for the current owner). But, you will also include a balloon payment in three years, allowing the owner a full exit if necessary.

The longer term (7 years) gives you breathing room by making your payment affordable (the longer the term, the lower the payment). The balloon payment (meaning that even though the loan amortizes over 7 years, the remaining balance after 3 years will be due in full) gives the current owner a way out in a short period as well as provides you time (3 years) to establish yourself in the business. When the time does come, you have a track record that you can take to the bank to finance that balloon balance. Plus, if both of you are happy with the way things are going; you can always refinance the balance (balloon) with the current owner at the 3 year anniversary date.

Now, if agreed, you get the business (what you were working for to begin with). The current owner not only sells the business; but given our example above, earns $22,700 in interest above the original purchase price; interest that you would have paid to the bank anyway if you were approved for a bank loan. Might as well pay it to the current owner.

From our example, your monthly payment would be around $1,500 a month; very affordable and at the 3 year balloon date. The remaining balance would be approximately $60,000; much easier to get a loan approved for than the original $100,000.

In the end, you, as the new business owner are no worse off and now have bought yourself some time to show both the selling business owner and the banks that you are a true success.

As we know acquisition financing for small businesses can be difficult. This is particularly true where there are no significant tangible assets that the banks will recognise as security.

Many deals fall over due to both the owner and the purchaser not fully understanding the range of payment terms that are available to them.

As the European and American population are ageing and more businesses go on the market for sale, 'owner financing' is becoming an increasingly popular method for buying and selling businesses.

Another scenario is seeing the seller who, for example, is profiting $500,000 per annum looking to sell the business for $1,000,000. As part of the 'owner finance' arrangement, the seller will give the buyer two years to pay off the $1,000,000, meaning the buyer will ultimately pay off the entire acquisition price out of the profits of the newly acquired company.

Owner finance is simply a method of purchasing a business whereby the agreed purchase price forms a loan between owner and purchaser, to be repaid out of the ongoing profits of the business.

To align the interests of both parties and ensure the purchaser is incentivised to pay off the loan as quickly as possible, there will often be an interest rate attached to the loan that will typically be between 5-10 per cent per annum.

In this example the owner is effectively loaning the money to the buyer, in order to ensure the transaction goes ahead and the business gets sold.

The caveat for this is that if the purchaser defaults on a loan repayment, depending on the terms of the owner loan, the original owner may have the right to take back the business or specified assets of the business. This scenario isn't good for either party, usually with both doing everything they can to avoid it.

Often the owner will request a portion of the sale price upfront, with the remainder of the balance to be paid over time. With this example, the owner might request 10 per cent upfront, with the remaining 90 per cent to be paid on owner finance terms.

In this instance, the purchaser can raise the upfront component from a private equity investor who may fund the initial 10 per cent in exchange for 10 per cent of the business. Provided the acquisition target is a robust business, it will be easier to raise private money for an acquisition than it is for a startup venture.

This is a common funding mechanism as it allows the purchaser to engage "smart money" that can add value to the business, while still acquiring 90 per cent of a business using none of their own money.

You might ask, would a current business owner, looking to get out of the business, be willing to agree to owner finance?

Two main reasons why the answer is yes.

1. The business owner, given the recent economy condition and the fact that banks are not lending, might not be able to sell the business any other way.

2. The business owner benefits additionally as he/she receives not only the principal from the loan (what they wanted in the first place) but will also earn interest from the financing as your interest payments go to them and not the bank (e.g. major selling point).

In good times, for a business to succeed, the business owner has to be creative in all aspects of the business. In bad times, like now, to be a successful business owner, you have to get doubly creative, especially when it comes to financing.

If you have no other choice or options, it never hurts to go to the current owner and ask them to finance the purchase; what do you really have to lose? Just come prepare with a deal that benefits both you and the owner because owner financing just might be the best and last way to finance a business purchase today.

Chapter 11: Using Credit Cards to Fund Your New Business.

Credit cards can provide easy money for young, growing companies. But they also come with serious dangers.

How it works: There are personal credit cards, and there are cards tailored toward small businesses. Each come with benefits and rewards. There are more government protections for personal credit card holders, while business cards can have higher limits and rewards such as discounted office supplies that are tailored toward business owners.

No matter what, you will wreck your personal finances if the bills aren't paid, so don't be tricked into thinking you need to use a business card with the business.

Upside: Besides providing needed cash flow to young businesses, credit cards can also improve credit scores for owners and businesses alike; as long as payments are made on time. There are also special rewards and perks such as airline miles, discounted gas or even cash.

The funds are also easier to come by, which can help in a pinch.

Embracing business credit cards for daily expenses inside the business can also aid in record keeping by helping business owners to separate personal and business finances, track employee spending, reduce time balancing cheque books, and produce business financial reports.

Downside: Credit card interest rates are much higher than traditional loans, which can make them a pricey form of debt that will drag the business down during tough times.

A research found that for every $1,000 in credit-card debt that a small business takes on, its chances of long-term survival fall by more than 2 percent.

For a young company, it is crucial to tap personal funds, family, friends and other investors in order to avoid racking up too much credit card debt. Such high-interest debt will swallow up a young company's revenues.

Getting late on a payments and you can damage your credit score, hurting your ability to take out loans as the business grows. A late payment on a small business credit card also gets you reported to a business credit bureau.

You could get burned on a small business credit card if you don't scrutinize the fine print and ask a lot of questions. Such cards are not covered by the 2009 Credit Card Accountability, Responsibility and Disclosure Act. The law protects consumers from such practices as arbitrary interest-rate increases.

If you think you won't be able to pay off purchases in a single billing period, it might be better to charge them on the personal credit card, rather than a business card.

Don't just hone in on annual fees. Check out baggage insurance, concierge service, employee-expense tracking, and even access to airline clubs.

Search out the business cards with the best rewards in order to make something back on the business' purchases.

Take advantage of introductory zero-percent rates on both purchases and balance transfers.

Use different types of cards for different types of transactions. For example, a business-rewards credit card might be best for everyday expenses, while a zero-interest personal card might be the best for funding.

Chapter 12: Raising Money From Friends and Family.

It is one of the most common forms of business funding out there. Banks and independent investors might not want to risk money on you. But those who are close to you and believe in you might be willing to take a chance on your fledgling business.

Upside: This is your best chance to secure money to get the business off the ground. If your friends and relatives don't want to give you money, who will? If one or a few of them has business savvy, better yet. Bringing them on as investors transforms them into motivated advisors. Plus, they will likely be more forgiving than outside investors when it comes to your business' ups and downs.

Raising money from your personal network can also be a step toward securing money from future investors, because it demonstrates that you are grounded in a network of family and acquaintances who have already bought into the business plan.

Downside: You risk lost friends and strained relationships with relatives. Your next holiday party won't be as fun if half of the people there think you fleeced them on a failed business venture, or are annoyed because you went on vacation before paying their money back.

That is why it is best not to get too informal about the business relationship. Be upfront about risks, lay out the business plan that the money will fund, and put the rules behind the investment in writing.

How it works: It could be a gift, a loan or an equity investment in the business. Each have pluses and minuses, and each should be recorded in writing, in many cases a legal document.

Gifts: The great thing about a gift is that you don't have to pay it back. But you probably won't raise as much as you would if you were offering a potential return on the money. Also, gifts can quickly turn into loans in the minds of friends and relatives should you succeed. A signed document, even a letter saying the money was given, will protect you down the road.

Loans: Many experts suggest loans as the optimal way for friends and family to invest because there are set repayment terms. They will know how long it will take for them to get their money back and at what interest. A business attorney can easily draw up a "promissory note" detailing the terms of the loan.

The downside of borrowing is that you are tying up some of your business' cash flow in the repayments.

Equity: You don't have to pay them until you make a profit or cash out, but you are literally turning a friend or a relative into a business partner if you give them an ownership stake in the company. You will want a business lawyer involved in this.

Consider if you want this person as a business partner? He or she will have a right to tell you how to run the venture. This can be highly beneficial if your acquaintance/investor has entrepreneurial experience or other useful know-how. But it can quickly become an annoyance otherwise. You also risk straining the relationship should you move on to another venture.

How to get it: It is always advisable to present a formal business plan when pitching to prospective investors even friends and relatives. But unlike in other cases, you don't need to present printed materials and charts up front. Rather, it is best to lay out your business plans verbally, because those in your personal network will likely base their decision on trust.

The "kitchen table pitch" is really about selling yourself. Be frank about the risks, and explain what the money will go toward and how it will grow the business. Then follow up with written materials later.

Most entrepreneurs have learned that it's almost always quicker and easier to get cash from someone you know, rather than angel investors or professional investors. In fact, most investors "require" that you already have some investment from friends and family before they will even step up to the plate.

You see, investors invest in people, before they invest in ideas or products. Since they don't know you (yet), their first integrity check on you as a person is whether your friends and family believe in you strongly enough to give you seed money for your new idea. If they won't do it, then why would I a stranger invest in you?

Friends and family will likely not expect the same level of sophistication on the business model and financials as a professional investor, but they do expect to see certain things. Here is a summary of some key items to think about as an entrepreneur before approaching friends, family, or even fools.

1. Don't be afraid to ask, carefully.

If you seat around quietly waiting for someone you know to offer you money to fund a startup, you will probably have a long wait.

On the other hand, if you open every conversation with "I need money," you won't have any friends or any money. Practice your "elevator pitch," and end it by asking for the order.

2. Be upbeat and respectful.

Nothing kills everyone's optimism and desire to help quicker than a negative or arrogant attitude.

If they are going to put cash into your company, chances are that they will expect to spend a fair amount of time together, either helping you or certainly discussing progress. Nobody likes a downer.

3. Be passionate about the idea.

Friends and family will quickly detect your level of sincerity and thought behind the idea.

You need to convince them that you have been working on this vision for a long time, and have done the "due diligence" on all the potential knockoffs. Daydreams and "the idea of the moment" won't get much respect.

4. Demonstrate progress and your own "skin in the game"

Saying that you need money to start is not nearly as convincing as saying that you have built a prototype on your own dime, but need more to roll it out.

We all know people who can talk a good game, but never get around to building anything.

5. Ask for the minimum rather than the maximum.

We would all love to have a million dollars of funding to "do it right" and build the company of our dreams. But your chances are minimal of finding someone who will give you that much to start.

Set some milestones for three or four months out, and show what you can do, then ask for more.

6. Communicate the risks, and write down the agreement.

Be honest with naïve family members and friends about the inherent risks of a buying a business; at least high percent fail in the first five years.

Don't take money from family or friends who can't afford to lose it. Think hard about the consequences of a possible business failure and the loss of their funding.

7. Show some incremental value along the way.

Look for ways to get some traction with a minimal product, while you are still developing the main event.

In high technology, this is called "release early and iterate," which allows you to make corrections as you go, as well as adjust for the market changes. It also shows progress to early backers.

8. Network to build investor relationships before you ask for money.

Having a real project, rather than just an idea, is a strong positive when networking for angels investor. Now you really have something to discuss, and real credibility as an entrepreneur.

Build the relationship first, ask for advice on a real project, then maybe money later.

9. Don't think of friends and family funding only as a last resort.

Overall, don't think of friends and family funding only as a last resort. There are massive advantages, like sharing profits with friends and family, as well as the strategic credibility that can be gained from funding from someone you know, rather than from a professional investor.

I hope all of these points seem like common sense to you, and you wouldn't think of handling it any other way. Yet, I am continually amazed at how often I am approached as a professional investor by strangers asking for a million dollars to fund an idea, without hitting even one of the above points. We can all recount horror stories of families and friendships torn apart by money lost on someone else's speculative dream. In these cases both the entrepreneur and the funding partner are the fools. Don't be one.

Chapter 13: Crowdfunding

Crowdfunding is about persuading individuals to each give you a small donation; $10, $50, $100, maybe more. Once you get thousands of donors, you have some serious cash on hand.

This has all become possible in recent years thanks to a proliferation of websites that allow nonprofits, artists, musicians and yes, businesses to raise money. This is the social media version of fundraising.

There are more than 600 crowdfunding platforms around the world, with fundraising reaching billions of dollars annually, according to a recent research.

How it works: The most common type of crowdfunding fundraising is using sites like Kickstarter and Indiegogo variety, where donations are sought in return for special rewards. That could mean free product or even a chance to be involved in designing the product or service.

It is also possible to use crowdfunding to assemble loans and royalty financing. The site Lending Club, for example, allows members to directly invest in and borrow from each other, with the claim that eliminating the banking middleman means "both sides can win" in the transactions. Royalty financing sites appear to be more rare, but the idea is to link business owners with investors who lend money for a guaranteed percentage of revenues for whatever the business is selling.

The holy grail is to sell company shares or ownership stakes in the company on crowdfunding sites, because it could be like a mini-IPO without the traditional hurdles. In the past, this has only been legal with accredited investors, people who each have more than $1 million in net worth or more than $200,000 in annual income.

The good news is that the Jumpstart Our Business Startups Act of 2012 allows stock to be sold to the general public over crowdfunding sites, but as of mid-2013, the SEC was still hammering out the rules.

Upside: Crowdfunding provides another strategy early stage companies ready to take it to the next level; such as rolling out a product or service. Before, a business owner was subject to the caprices of individual angel investors or bank loan officers. Now it is possible to pitch a business plan to the masses.

A successful crowdfunding round not only provides your business with needed cash, but creates a base of customers who feel as though they have a stake in the business' success.

Downside: If you don't have an engaging story to tell, then your crowdfunding bid could be a flop. Sites such as Kickstarter don't collect money until a fundraising goal is reached, so that is still a lot of wasted time that could have been spent doing other things to grow the business.

It could be even worse if you meet your goal but then realize you underestimated how much money you needed. A business risks getting sued if it promises customers products or perks in return for donations, and then fails to deliver.

There is also an argument to be made that angel investors and even bank officers provide more than just money. They provide entrepreneurs with needed advice. Business owners miss out on such mentorship when they ignore traditional investors and turn to the crowd.

Here are more factors that can better ensure a successful crowdfunding campaign.

1. Have at least a small network of enthusiastic friends and family willing to help get the ball rolling by giving and urging others to give.

2. If you are giving out perks in return for money, make sure the perks are good.

3. Present a serious business plan and an explanation of why the money will take your enterprise to the next level.

4. Demonstrate that you have your own skin in the game because of the personal funds you have already poured into the business.

5. Include a video pitch and keep it short and concise, with a call to action.

6. Include different rewards for different levels of giving.

7. Be prepared to essentially live online, staying active on social media sites, until the crowdfunding campaign is complete.

Chapter 14: Taking Ownership Without a Major Down Payment.

If you have been thinking about starting a business or expanding your current venture, you will be pleased to know that obtaining financing for a business can be quite simple. Some say it is much easier to get this money when you are buying an existing business than starting a new one; in fact many people have been buying a business with no money. This may seem impossible, especially with banks tightening their guidelines for granting business loans, but there are plenty of ways to work around that.

No matter how experienced you are with structuring a business deal, there is always something new to be learned. Entrepreneurs who have been forced to go without the help of a traditional lender have learned a lot about buying a business with no money, or only a little money down. Gone are the days when the bank down the street will welcome a newly minted MBA with open arms and an open mind. Unless you are prepared to collateralize the loan with personal liquid assets, they are not going to grant a loan, and even if they did the terms they offer are not as business-friendly as they sound.

Seller-Assisted Financing.

More so than ever, the vast majority of business acquisitions involve some degree of seller financing. In fact, with small businesses it is estimated that more than 80 percent will get some form of financial aid from the current owner, often adding up to 50 percent of the purchase price. By providing financing, the seller validates the potential and viability of the business, making it appear less risky to the buyer. By funding a portion of the acquisition, owners often get a higher selling price because the buyer recognizes that the seller is also taking a risk with the transaction. Buyers feel more comfortable with this arrangement because it serves as reinforcement that the seller's claims about the business were true.

Small Business Association (SBA) Financing.

Contrary to popular belief, the SBA does not lend money to people who want to buy a business; however, it does guarantee loans for small business acquisitions. The guaranteed loans offer up to $1.3 million and possibly more if the deal includes real estate. Terms are usually favourable and up to ten years for most traditional loans, but you may need at least 25 percent equity on your home in order to fully collateralize the loan. Unfortunately, most small business acquisitions do not meet the SBA guidelines because the review uses the weakest of your past two or three tax returns.

Buying a business with no money may not be a possibility for everyone, but if you are able to purchase an existing business, get 50 percent seller financing and fully collateralize an SBA-guaranteed loan, it's possible to take ownership without a major down payment.

Chapter 15: How to Structure an Earn-out.

When there is a valuation difference between what a buyer thinks a business is worth and what the seller expects to profit, an earn-out can bridge that gap. Here is how to make a deal that is good for both parties.

What is the value of your business? That depends on whom you ask. Ask potential buyers, especially when they are being cautious in tough economic times, and it might not meet your expectations.

Negotiating a sale of a privately-held business is never a breeze and it's much less so in a down market in which there is little competition among buyers to drive up the multiple. When a seller's expectations are not being met by potential buyers, including an earn-out provision in the acquisition contract can help narrow the price-expectation divide.

A common feature of many acquisitions, an earn-out stipulates that the original owners of a business are paid for the sale of their company, following which they are contractually obligated to stay with the company through a transition period, and they are provided with the incentive to have a demonstrable effect on the company's financial performance going forward. Achieving or exceeding a certain level of performance; criteria are typically set over a period of several years; means the original owners will earn a much larger profit from the sale. For buyers, an earn-out can offer the owner protection against overpaying for a company that does not end up thriving or growing in the way its original owners expected. It can also smooth the period of ownership transition.

Call it an incentive; call it delayed gratification; call it a compromise. Earn-outs can benefit both buyers and sellers.

It's a way for the buyer to put some skin in the game for the seller after the deal closes, and to provide some financial incentive for them to work hard in terms of the company's business after they close the deal. In a situation where the seller might believe there is a great opportunity for future growth potential, they can take some added benefit in the transaction.

Setting Realistic Expectations.

When there is a gap between an owner and a potential acquirer in the perceived value of a business, it is usually caused by the expected future growth of the company. That is only natural; but as a small business owner, it's necessary to step back and ask yourself; If your expectations are higher than those of your buyer, why is that?

After all, it's commonly known that roughly three-quarters of all mergers and acquisitions fall short of the expectations that are stated when the deal is announced and about half of all deals result in a loss of value for the buyer's shareholders. So, analyze exactly what you are optimistic about and how much of your purchase price you are willing to risk on being successful in the future.

Being equipped with solid expectations for your businesses success over the next five years can prepare you well for negotiating an earn-out.

Consider next what portion of your asking price you did be willing to risk and work for in the future.

An earn-out is a contingent payout, which essentially involves shifting some of the purchase price to be paid in the future on the realization of future earnings or some other benchmarks of success. So the owner needs to be willing to delay some of the price and be aware they might never get it; because most earn-out clauses are tied to the company's performance (measured in sales, earnings, or some other benchmark) over a three-to-five-year period, that is the timeline you should be thinking about your company's health within before embarking on negotiations. If your company had a track-record of performing at or exceeding forecasts in the past, this fact should give you added negotiating power.

Knowing expectations is vital is because the range of earn-out terms that could be offered is vast. A buyer might agree to pay 90 percent of the total purchase price you desire upfront with the remaining 10 percent paid in stock or cash after a year of earn-out time. Alternately, the buyer might split the sale price 50/50 over five years during which time the owner must agree to stay with the company and optimize its performance.

When Disney acquired Club Penguin in 2007, for example, it paid $350 million upfront, with $350 million more promised through a series of earn-outs. For high-tech and service businesses with high-growth potential, a typical deal might include an upfront payment from an acquirer of between 60 and 80 percent, with the balance paid over time possibly as an earn-out tied to performance.

It is estimated that, in the post-dot-com-boom era, the owners of private companies regularly have been taking between 40 and 45 percent of the total pay-out through an earn-out agreement, according to surveys. If you are embarking on a sale, you will want to make sure you know their future involvement is worthwhile and is the best way to spend time for the money offered.

Keeping it Simple.

For entrepreneurs looking for a quick sale of their business, the most simple earn-out is none at all. There are significant risks involved in any acquisition that involves future conditions; especially when the old owner is expected to come on board to work for someone else and live by their rules.

A CEO must recognize they will not be in control of their own destiny in any part the same way they were. They will have new bosses and will have to march to a new set of rules than they had to when it was their own company.

Many earn-outs depend on an extremely complicated matrix of variables and goals. This should be avoided if possible. Earn-outs are most effective as an incentive for the seller when the size of the payout is determined based upon one or two simple variables. A buyer who constructed a complicated set of goals covering earnings, customer retention, and myriad other circumstances should be challenged. These conditions might not be fully under your control should you accept the earn-out and too many variables especially when some are out of your hands can make achieving your earn-out impossible.

What you don't want to happen is to make it so they control you and that you don't make your earn-out; that can be that they control some marketing expenses or some other element that would change the game for you and take any control of the situation out of your hands within a year or so out.

In order to avoid spending years of your life working on a possibly unattainable goal, you will want to enter acquisition negotiations armed with a legal counsel, as well as financial advisors, specializing in mergers and acquisitions. Instruct them to fight for a simple deal with an earn-out based on an easy-to-quantify metric, such as higher corporate revenue or an expanded client base.

The simplest earn-out might be a model newly being set by Google. The search giant's director of corporate development told the Wall Street Journal that though the company used to be "addicted to" earn-outs and milestone-based compensation, the company is now shying away from such practices. Identifying myriad benchmarks and determining fair pricing for the earn-outs proved to be just too difficult. Now, 'we tend to have pretty generous packages but they are time-based, whether in equity or cash, instead of specific milestones,' Google's David Sobota told the paper.

Aiming for simplicity is best, too, for the future relationship between a company and its new owners. With aligned incentives and clear objectives, you will have less cause for arguing or potential legal squabbles when it's time for your payout.

Avoid Earn-out Burn-out.

Just as simplicity is key, for the seller, staying true to your priorities as a business owner is equally important. Sure, if you believe strongly in your company's potential, and want to guide its success through new ownership, an earn-out might give you the opportunity to do so. But ensuring that a few key elements are in place in your agreement can greatly strengthen the new arrangement.

1. Keep your key players. If other executives were integral to your company's growth and success, will your company be able to function under new ownership without them? If not, come up with deals to lock them in, too.

2. Keep the length of your contract as short as possible. It sounds obvious, but you will minimize the potential for burn-out by minimizing your time working with your new parent company. You can always renew and re-negotiate, but can't hit undo. It's that simple.

3. Make sure you have control. Ensure that the contract expressly states that you will oversee any departments that will be executing on the goals and standards set forth in the earn-out. You should never allow yourself to be accountable for what you cannot control.

4. Ensure that incentives are in place. You know what motivates you at work. One is seeing your business succeed, and the second is money. If you have made a lot of cash in the initial sale, it's natural to lose attachment to future goals for the company. The earn-out percentage should be high enough to keep you from losing interest, especially in the event of a setback. If you are going to commit, commit fully.

Each of these standards, which you and your buyer will negotiate, can and should be included in your earn-out agreement. To vet that document, enlist acquisition specialists on both the legal and financial front. Both buyers and sellers should expect to pay top-dollar for acquisition services, though, due to the complex nature of the work. In no case should the buyer be the only voice in determining any of these elements.

In downstream earn-outs you have to be very, very careful; know the people that you are dealing with on the other side of the table, and work very hard to get the incentives aligned for all of the parties.

Ensure Good Chances for Success (and Avoid Disaster).

You already know the importance of laying out simple, clear-cut standards that must be met for an earn-out to pay-out. There are some additional questions both parties should consider before signing on the dotted line.

1. Will the acquired party have enough autonomy?

Earn-outs tend to work well when the seller is going to continue to run pretty much as before. To that end, a seller should get in writing the seller's commitment to leave operations largely unchanged. If certain redundancies or back-office functions are to be folded into the acquiring company, that is fine. You simply want to make sure that every part of the acquired company that can be run independently is run independently.

2. Is the purpose of the earn-out financial or strategic?

An earn-out can be made for purely financial reasons, or a buyer can be making a bet on the owner's ability to expand the business. You will want to know which motivation is at play and whether it is likely to change after the deal is closed. If the acquirer keeps a respectful distance and seems to be giving you autonomy, that is a good sign.

3. Who is the umpire? How will progress against an earn-out's goals be evaluated?

Consider both who will be evaluating the entrepreneur's performance under new ownership, and when evaluations will take place. Is it simply at the end of the period set in the contract, or will progress be tracked quarterly? Will the earn-out be allocated piecemeal or in one lump-sum? There is no right answer, but these questions should be addressed early on in your negotiations.

4. What will happen in the event outside factors drastically change the outcome?

Factors in neither party's control can harm the buyer's and entrepreneur's ability to maximize the rewards pledged in an earn-out. What if your industry tanks? What if a natural disaster hits? What if your biggest client was Lehman Brothers or Bear Stearns? Make sure to create contingency plans to address the most unlikely of scenarios especially if you are entering into a long-term earn-out deal.

Chapter 16: Paying Too Much for Acquisition.

Despite 30 years of evidence demonstrating that most acquisitions don't create value for the acquiring company's shareholders, executives continue to make more deals, and bigger deals, every year. Recent research shows that acquisitions in the 1990s have just as poor a record as they did in the 1970s. There are plenty of reasons for this poor performance; irrational exuberance about the strategic importance of the deal, enthusiasm built up during the excitement of negotiations, and weak integration skills, to name a few. Many failures occur, though, simply because the acquiring company paid too much for the acquisition.

It wasn't a good deal on the day it was made and it never will be. A good example is Quaker Oats' acquisition of Snapple. Some industry analysts estimated that the $1.7 billion purchase price was as much as $1 billion too much. The stock price of both companies declined the day the deal was announced. Problems with implementation and a downturn in the market for New Age drinks quickly led to performance problems. Just 28 months later, Quaker sold Snapple to Triarc Companies for less than 20% of what it had paid. Quaker Oats' and Triarc's stock prices went up the day that deal was announced.

How should you think about what to pay for an acquisition and how should you know when to walk away? In the course of a research project on mergers and acquisitions, we explored those questions with 75 senior executives from 40 companies. All were experienced, skilled acquirers. We learned that there is a systematic way for senior managers to think about pricing acquisitions. We also learned that even experienced acquirers, who should know better, sometimes get too attached to a deal. When that happens, it's essential to have organizational disciplines in place that will rein in the emotion. A combination of analytical rigor and strict process discipline will help senior executives and board members guide their companies toward the right acquisitions at the right price.

No Single, Correct Price.

It's tempting to think that the reason so many acquisitions are overpriced is straightforward; just that most deals today are too rich, that executives routinely get caught up in the excitement of the race and offer more than they should. Indeed, that is often the case. But it's not always so simple. In fact, the relationship between the size of the premium and the success of the deal is not linear. Deals with Low Premiums Often Fail and Vice Versa. In half the cases, the acquirer paid a low premium, and the total return on investment one year later was negative. In the other half, the acquirer paid a high premium, yet total return one year later was positive.

The question, then, is not whether an acquirer has paid too high a price in an absolute sense. Rather, it's whether an acquirer has paid more than the acquisition was worth to that particular company.

What one company can afford will differ from what another company can afford and, more than likely, from the asking price. Ultimately, the key to success in buying another company is knowing the maximum price you can pay and then having the discipline not to pay a penny more.

The bidding war that Bell Atlantic and Vodafone waged to acquire Air-Touch Communications illustrates the point that the right price is relative; that is, there is no single correct price for an acquisition. Rumours that Bell Atlantic was in negotiations to acquire AirTouch first surfaced on December 31, 1998. The terms of the Bell Atlantic bid were publicized four days later; it had offered $73 per share, or $45 billion, a 7% premium above Air-Touch's closing share price a week earlier of $68. Bell Atlantic's stock price immediately declined by 5%. Clearly, the market did not like the deal.

Vodafone entered the fray on January 7 with a bid of around $55 billion, or $89 per share. Negotiations continued for the next several days until, on January 15, Vodafone agreed to pay $97 per share, for a total of $62 billion. That price was 33% more than Bell Atlantic's original offer and 43% more than AirTouch's share price before the first rumours of Bell Atlantic's offer had surfaced. Implicit in the deal was the fact that for its shareholders to break-even, Vodafone would have to find cost savings and revenue generators worth at least $20 billion. Yet the market liked this deal very much. During the course of this bidding war, Vodafone's stock price actually increased some 14%.

What explains the market's negative reaction to Bell Atlantic's modest premium and its positive reaction to Vodafone's high premium? The answer is that acquiring AirTouch created more valuable synergies for Vodafone than it would have for Bell Atlantic. First of all, Vodafone had a much larger share of the cellular market than Bell Atlantic did in Europe and as it happened, Vodafone was strong in European countries where AirTouch was not; the two companies complemented each other extremely well. Together, they would create the first complete pan-European cellular telephone company. As a result, they would be able to save a tremendous amount in roaming fees paid to other cellular operators and in interconnection fees paid to fixed line operators. By contrast, a Bell Atlantic - AirTouch combination would not have created a pan-European company, so it had far less potential.

More Deals, More Failures.

Pricing an acquisition correctly is extraordinarily important given how many deals there are and how many fail. During the past decade, merger and acquisition activity has steadily increased, as measured both by the total number of deals and by the value of those deals. In 1998 alone, 20,448 deals were completed worth a total of $2 trillion.

The prognosis for most of those deals is not good. Several studies covering merger and acquisition activity in the past 75 years have concluded that well over half of mergers and acquisitions failed to create their expected value. In many cases, value was destroyed, and the company's performance after the deal was significantly below what it had been before the deal. The success rate is not much better today than it was 75 years ago, despite numerous, well-publicized studies illuminating the high failure rates.

The executives who continue to make bad deals don't appear to have learned much. The equity markets, by contrast, have learned from experience. We studied 131 deals, each valued at $500 million or more, that took place between 1994 and 1997 in the United States, Europe, and Asia. Our analysis, consistent with earlier study of U.S. companies, shows that in 59% of the deals, the total market-adjusted return of the acquiring company went down on announcement.

That means the market thought the deal would destroy rather than create value for the shareholders of the acquiring or merged company. Returns for 71% of those deals were negative over the next 12 months. By contrast, of the 41% of deals where the total return went up on announcement in other words, where the market expected value to be created; 55% still had positive returns in the ensuing year. This analysis demonstrates both that most deals do not create value and that the market is fairly good at predicting which ones will and which ones won't.

Another source of synergy in the Vodafone-AirTouch deal was the anticipated savings from high-volume purchases of equipment such as handsets, switches, and base stations, which the two companies were already basing on the same technology and buying from the same suppliers. Those savings have been estimated at $330 million, starting in 2002. Finally, having a common European currency will allow Vodafone to use a pan-European flat-rate pricing plan. Should it move in that direction, Vodafone will put tremendous pressure on competitors operating only within each European country. Such rivals would be forced to respond through complicated joint ventures or consolidations. While its competitors engage in these time-consuming and expensive activities, Vodafone would have already digested its acquisition of AirTouch and be one step ahead of the game.

As this example shows, there may be a vast difference between the price one company can pay for an acquisition and the price another can pay. Often the two companies are direct competitors. When they are, the company that can least afford it will be sorely tempted to ignore the financial case and overpay. To do so is nearly always a mistake.

Pricing the Deal.

Managers and board members judging the merits of a proposed acquisition need to understand several distinct concepts of value. What is the True Value of an Acquisition? In today's market, the purchase price of an acquisition will nearly always be higher than the intrinsic value of the target company. An acquirer needs to be sure that there are enough cost savings and revenue generators, synergy and value to justify the premium so that the target company's shareholders don't get all the value the deal creates.

Intrinsic Value.

The most basic value of the company, its intrinsic value, is based principally on the net present value of expected future cash flows completely independent of any acquisition. That assumes the company continues under current management with whatever revenue growth and performance improvements have already been anticipated by the market. AirTouch's intrinsic value was around $68 per share just before Bell Atlantic's bid.

Market Value.

On top of the intrinsic value, the market may add a premium to reflect the likelihood that an offer for the company will be made (or a higher offer will be tendered than one currently on the table). Market value commonly called "current market capitalization" is the same as the share price; it reflects the market participants' valuation of the company. For AirTouch, the market value was $73 per share on December 31, the day the press first reported that a deal with Bell Atlantic was in the works.

Purchase Price.

Wall Street calls this the "anticipated takeout value." It's the price that a bidder anticipates having to pay to be accepted by the target shareholders. For AirTouch, the purchase price turned out to be $97 per share, representing a premium of $29 a share over its intrinsic value.

Synergy Value.

The net present value of the cash flows that will result from improvements made when the companies are combined. These are improvements above and beyond those the market already anticipates each company would make if the acquisition didn't occur, since those are already incorporated into the intrinsic value of each company. Based on the deal price, Vodafone's estimated synergy value was at least $20 billion.

Value Gap.

The difference between the intrinsic value and the purchase price.

In today's market, both the acquirer and the target company know that the purchase price will be higher than the intrinsic value; in other words, that the buyer will most likely pay a premium. That premium allocates some of the future benefits of the combination to the target shareholders. Absent a premium, most target shareholders would refuse to sell. The acquirer's managers need to figure out just how large a value gap their company can bridge through synergies. The target, meanwhile, will second-guess the acquirer, trying to calculate how high the price can be pushed. If there is more than one potential acquirer and the bidding gets competitive, that places even more upward pressure on the price.

Calculating Synergy Value.

There are two keys to success in pricing an acquisition. The first is to make sure that those individuals calculating a target's synergy value are rigorous and that they work with realistic assumptions. The second is to ensure that the acquirer pays no more than it should, no matter how many arm-waving arguments are aired to the effect that "this is a strategic deal; we did be crazy not to do it!"

Acquirers generally base their calculations on five types of synergies; cost savings, revenue enhancements, process improvements, financial engineering, and tax benefits. The value of each type of synergy will depend on the particular skills and circumstances of the acquirer, something vividly illustrated by the different amounts that Bell Atlantic and Vodafone bid for AirTouch and the market's reaction to those bids.

Cost Savings.

This is the most common type of synergy and the easiest to estimate. Cost savings is "hard synergies" the level of certainty that they will be achieved is quite high. Usually, they come from eliminating jobs, facilities, and related expenses that are no longer needed when functions are consolidated, or they come from economies of scale in purchasing. Cost savings are likely to be especially large when one company acquires another from the same industry in the same country. For example, SBC

Communications, the former Southwestern Bell, realized substantial cost savings when it acquired Pacific Telesis. Within the first two years of this merger, SBC saved more than $200 million in information-technology operating and maintenance costs. It also saved tens of millions of dollars by combining the merged companies' purchasing power.

Even though cost savings are the easiest synergy to calculate, overly optimistic projections certainly do occur, so you need to look very carefully at the numbers you are presented with. If you are evaluating projections, be aware of three common problems. First, analysts may overlook the fact that definitions of cost categories vary from company to company. (For example, are warranty costs included in the cost of production or the cost of sales?) So it may appear that there are more easily eliminated costs in a category than turn out to be the case. Second, costs are incurred in different places depending on the structure of each company. Acquirers may assume they can eliminate more corporate or divisional administrative costs than they actually can because essential work is getting done in unexpected places. Third, it is easier to eliminate positions than the people who fill them. Often a job is eliminated on paper, but the person in the job is very talented and must be shifted elsewhere in the company. Therefore, if a consolidation seems to suggest that 200 jobs are destined to go, that doesn't mean that 200 salaries are, too.

Acquirers often underestimate how long it will take to realize cost savings. Sometimes that happens because the plans specifying how integration will proceed are insufficiently detailed. In other cases, it happens because the people in both companies are resistant to change, and senior managers often delay making tough cost-cutting decisions and, of course, the longer it takes for cost savings to be realized, the less value they create.

Revenue Enhancements.

It's sometimes possible for an acquirer and its target to achieve a higher level of sales growth together than either company could on its own. Revenue enhancements are notoriously hard to estimate, however, because they involve external variables beyond management's control. The customer base of the acquired company, for instance, may react negatively to different prices and product features. A combined customer base may balk at making too many purchases from a single supplier and competitors may lower their prices in response to an acquisition. Revenue enhancements are so difficult to predict, in fact, that some wise companies don't even include them when calculating synergy value. A friend of mine says, "We model this (revenue enhancements), but never factor it into the price." Similarly, I consider them "soft synergies" and discounts them heavily in calculations of synergy value.

Despite their dangers, revenue enhancements can create real value. Sometimes the target brings a superior or complementary product to the more extensive distribution channel of the acquirer. That happened when Lloyds TSB acquired the Cheltenham and Gloucester Building Society (which had a better home-loan product) and Abbey Life (which had insurance products). In both cases, Lloyds TSB was able to sell those products to its dramatically larger retail customer base, thus generating more revenue than the three entities could have done individually. Similarly, having acquired Duracell for a 20% premium, Gillette was confirmed in its expectation that selling Duracell batteries through Gillette's existing channels for personal care products would increase sales, particularly internationally. Gillette sold Duracell products in 25 new markets in the first year after the acquisition and substantially increased sales in established international markets.

In other instances, a target company's distribution channel can be used to escalate the sales of the acquiring company's product. That occurred at Gillette when it acquired Parker Pen. In calculating what it could pay, Gillette estimated that it would be able to get an additional $25 million in sales for its own Waterman pens by taking advantage of Parker's distribution channels.

A final kind of revenue enhancement occurs when the bigger, post acquisition company gains sufficient critical mass to attract revenue neither company would have been able to realize alone. Consider what happened when ABN and AMRO merged to form ABN AMRO, the large Dutch bank. Afterward, other large banks pulled the new company in on syndicated loans that neither ABN nor AMRO would have been asked to participate in individually.

Process Improvements.

Cost savings result from eliminating duplication or from purchasing in volume; revenue enhancements are generated from combining different strengths from the two organizations. Process improvements, by contrast, occur when managers transfer best practices and core competencies from one company to another. That results in both cost savings and revenue enhancements.

The transfer of best practices can flow in either direction. The acquirer may buy a company because the target is especially good at something. Conversely, the acquirer may see that it can drastically improve the target's performance in a key area because of some competence the acquirer has already mastered.

Take the case of National Australia Bank's purchase of Florida mortgage lender HomeSide. HomeSide has an extremely efficient mortgage-servicing process that NAB plans to transfer to its banking operations in Australia, New Zealand, and the United Kingdom. The same was true of ABN AMRO when it acquired the U.S. commercial bank Standard and Federal. In that case, process improvements went hand in hand with cost savings: because its mortgage operation was so efficient, Standard and Federal eventually took over the combined bank's entire mortgage business.

Product development processes can also be improved so that new products can be produced at lower cost and get to market faster. Such was the case when Johnson Controls acquired Prince Corporation, a

105

maker of rear-view mirrors, door panels, visors, and other parts of automobile interiors. Prince was better than Johnson Controls at understanding customers' needs; both existing and anticipated and consequently it produced higher-margin products. Prince also had an excellent process for ramping up production of new products, which enabled it to move from design to mass production about twice as fast as Johnson Controls could, maintaining higher quality levels while speeding cycle times. Johnson learned from Prince and was soon able to apply those advantages to its own products.

For an example of the process improvements an acquiring company can bring to the table, take a look at newspaper giant Gannett. Gannett has a database of financial and nonfinancial measures for each of its 85 newspapers; executives use this rich resource to determine best practices, both boosting revenue and lowering costs. Gannett's CFO, explains, "We have been able to dramatically improve the papers we have bought. The key for us is knowing in very minute detail how to run a business. This gives us very specific ideas for improvement." Through more efficient production and distribution processes, Gannett has been able to extend its deadlines for news and advertising copy while simultaneously delivering the newspaper more quickly. That helps advertisers and improves Gannett's revenue. Gannett is also able to determine where classified rates are too high, hurting volume, and where they are too low, leaving money on the table. Because it can expect to yield quick, substantial process improvements, Gannett can pay very high premiums for its acquisitions. When you consider that many of the acquisitions are run independently and so don't offer many consolidation opportunities the high premiums are quite extraordinary. In fact, Gannett's CFO told us that, "People are often shocked at what we pay." In nearly all cases, though, performance improvements after the fact have justified the high prices.

The synergies of cost savings, revenue enhancements, and process improvements may be easy to understand conceptually, but our research demonstrates how hard they are to forecast accurately. Why? Most calculations of synergy value occur under horrendous conditions; time pressure is intense, information is limited, and confidentiality must be maintained. Since conditions are so far from ideal, the managers and board members responsible for the final decision should always scrutinize the assumptions underlying the numbers.

Financial Engineering.

Acquirers often think and hope that if they borrow cash to finance a transaction, they will reduce the weighted average cost of capital. That is not a good reason to do a deal. If either the acquirer or the target company could afford to take on more debt, each could have borrowed it on its own; however, some companies can find genuine synergies through financial engineering. For example, an acquisition can increase the size of a company to a level where there are clear economic benefits to pooling working-capital finance requirements and surplus cash, as well as netting currency positions. These benefits can be quite substantial. When the Credit Suisse Group merged with Winterthur, 10% of the forecasted synergies came from reducing funding costs through optimized capital management.

Here is another genuine financial-engineering synergy; a transaction may allow a company to refinance the target's debt at the acquirer's more favourable borrowing rate without affecting the acquirer's credit rating. That is especially likely to happen in the financial services sector because those companies are big and their risk is diversified.

Tax Benefits.

Tax considerations are often a barrier that must be overcome to justify a deal, a fact that makes tax-related synergies very difficult to assess. It's useful to distinguish between tax "structuring," which makes the deal possible, and tax "engineering" (also called tax planning), which ensures that the overall tax rate of the combined company is equal to or lower than the blended tax rates of the two companies before the deal. Regulators often believe that companies using perfectly legitimate structuring and engineering techniques to avoid incurring additional costs are simply taking advantage of loopholes. Thus companies are not anxious to disclose any clever techniques they may have used.

The goal of tax structuring is to avoid as many onetime tax costs as possible. Those costs may include capital and transfer duties, as well as change of ownership provisions that can trigger capital gains or prevent tax losses from being carried forward.

Assuming that analysts have identified structuring techniques that make the deal feasible, it is then possible to look for real tax-related synergies. One of the most common is the transfer of brands and other intellectual property to a low-tax subsidiary. But there are a host of other potential synergies; placing shared services and central purchasing in tax-advantaged locations; reorganizing within a country to pool taxes; pushing down debt into high-tax subsidiaries; and obtaining tax benefits that neither company could have realized on its own.

Even when real benefits can be obtained from tax engineering, companies should not make deals based on those benefits alone. The reason to pursue a merger or an acquisition is to achieve a better competitive position in the marketplace; a lower cost structure, for example, or a better platform for growth. While financial and tax-engineering tactics can produce value for shareholders, by themselves they do not strengthen a company's competitive position. Furthermore, the difficulty of integrating two companies can overwhelm purely financial and tax benefits.

Doing Deals for Strategic Reasons.

Assume that synergy value has been calculated extremely carefully and the numbers don't add up, but people in the company still claim there are compelling strategic reasons for doing the deal anyway. What next?

The most disciplined thing to do is walk away. If the numbers don't work, it is not a good deal. That is the practice at a company I use to work for. "We have a rule on the Executive Committee. When someone says 'strategic,' the rest of us say, 'too expensive.'"

Doubtless there are deals that should happen for strategic reasons even when the numbers don't sound promising, but they are few and far between. Before undertaking such an acquisition, senior managers should look with extraordinary rigor at the emotional state of those backing the deal and then at the strategic reasons themselves.

Doubtless there are deals that should happen for strategic reasons even when the numbers don't sound promising, but they are few and far between.

First, the emotional atmosphere. A lot of deals happen because managers fall in love with the idea of the deal. Successful executives, after all, are competitive people who hate to lose, and nothing brings out the competitive juices like going after another company, particularly when one's rivals are in hot pursuit. Anyone who has lived through a deal can tell you how exciting it can get. But as a friend of mine says, "You have to be careful not to let the thrill of the chase get the testosterone flowing."

Two of the most common arguments for ignoring the numbers are especially dangerous. When you hear someone say, "It's the last deal of its kind," beware. It's never the last deal. Deals fall apart all the time and what is more, divestitures are nearly as common as acquisitions in today's market. Assets unavailable today could easily be up for sale tomorrow.

Weak Links.

Our research focused on highly competent acquirers. Nevertheless, we have identified two areas that even these successful companies felt could be improved.

The first is risk analysis. Although, in the course of determining their bid price, all the companies we studied performed detailed financial and operating analyses, including sensitivity analysis, few of them did a rigorous risk analysis that examined what the least and most favourable outcomes could be. The downside analysis was particularly weak, given the built-in bias toward optimistic assumptions to make the numbers justify the deal.

When analyzing the downside, managers should ask themselves, "What could cause this deal to fail?" Depending on the industry and the country, that could be a dramatic and unanticipated new technology, a new nationalistic political regime, or new regulations resulting from a successful lawsuit. We suspect that in the future more companies will pay attention to this crucial task, particularly for very large deals. The analysis may well suggest that even when the probability of a disaster is low, if the consequences are very significant, the deal should not be done. The price of making a mistake is greater than the price of missing an opportunity.

The second area where even the best companies can improve their practices is in external communication to the capital markets, customers, suppliers, regulatory bodies, and geographic communities. Companies that have substantial M and A experience generally do a good job of communicating with employees, both before and after the deal closes; however, it is equally important to explain to external stakeholders what the benefits of the deal are and how the stakeholders will be affected, both positively and negatively.

The reason it's important that the capital markets understand the deal is obvious; their short-term reaction can make managers' lives miserable or delightful. Bob Bauman, who became CEO of Smith-Kline Beecham after it was formed from the merger of SmithKline Beckman and Beecham Group, felt that communication to the market was one weak spot in an otherwise very successful merger. "The marketplace has to have measures and lots of them. We gave them a lot of clarity about the end results we were aiming for, but insufficient detail on the milestones along the way. We could have done a better job here."

Bauman's comment reflects the importance of quantifying the value of expected synergies and reporting the progress made in achieving them. When that is done well, a company's credibility grows, which, in turn, is reflected in the stock price. Failure to communicate credibly will have the opposite effect.

The second argument is, "If you don't acquire a target, a major competitor will." But the fact is, if the numbers don't work for you, you should let your rival have the target company. Often that company will overpay and weaken its own competitive position. Better it than you!

If you feel compelled to move forward with a deal when the numbers tell you to stop, analyze the strategic reasons themselves as rigorously as you can. Remember that most strategic reasons to do deals boil down to some form of revenue generator or cost savings, which should be reflected in the numbers. Poke holes in the arguments and see if they still hold up. What could go wrong? What if the assumptions about the direction of technology and prices are wrong? What regulatory changes could make the deal fail, and how likely are they to occur? How could competitors react to the deal in ways that could hurt you even if they hurt themselves as well? Make sure that the group reviewing acquisition candidates includes strong sceptics with persuasive voices.

It may also make sense to introduce more sophisticated analytical techniques. Real-options valuation, for example, can help managers quantify potential, but not definite, future benefits.

That approach calculates a value for each of the options that the deal creates. Thus if the target company is developing a new, potentially valuable technology that could change the rules of competition in your industry, analysts can use real-options techniques to quantify the value of that technology based on a range of possible outcomes. For example, value can be realized by licensing the technology to others, by selling it off, or by investing in it further to develop a commercial product. Real-options thinking can also help managers identify the decisions they will have to make about future investments or other courses of action, and when those decisions need to be made.

Organizational Discipline and Pricing.

Successful acquiring companies know how to calculate synergy value, and they know how to walk away from a deal that seems fabulous until someone runs the numbers; however, they also know that sometimes human nature takes over in the heat of an exciting deal, and so they have developed process disciplines that help them stick to what the numbers tell them.

Many companies don't allow the negotiating manager to price the deal for fear that he or she will become too personally invested and overpay. Often a higher-level manager sets a price ceiling before negotiations begin; any negotiator or business-unit manager who wants to go over the ceiling must explain why and get explicit approval. Hutchison Whampoa and AlliedSignal both use that approach. In fact, AlliedSignal's CEO, at the time Larry Bossidy, has ultimate authority over all prices unless a deal is so large that it requires board approval.

The Interpublic Group of Companies (IPG) has a different approach to discipline. The large advertising and marketing-communications company has made more than 400 acquisitions; because the group has been so active, a lot of the pricing and negotiations have to occur at the business-unit level. The company has decreed that every target has to achieve at least a 12% return on investment within five to seven years. In addition, operating managers are required to meet operating targets within five years and those requirements are backed up with messages that managers understand. Says the company's, vice chairman of finance and operations, "Failure to meet these targets significantly lowers the long-term incentive awards our managers receive."

Frank Borelli, the CFO of Marsh & McLennan, has a good example of how strict process discipline can pay off. Within Marsh & McLennan, which offers insurance services, investment management, and human-resource-management consulting, Borelli is adamant about three criteria for doing any deal. The deal has to earn at least the company's cost of capital, it can't dilute earnings, and the target company's growth rate has to be higher than Marsh & McLennan's itself.

In the 1990s, the company had the chance to acquire two companies in the consolidating insurance-brokerage industry: Frank B. Hall in 1992 and Alexander and Alexander in 1996. The top managers in the insurance services unit were anxious to pursue both deals; however, neither company met all three criteria, and Borelli refused to bend the rules. The insurance services executives were dismayed when a major competitor, Aon, acquired both companies.

When an opportunity to buy Minet came along in late 1996, the insurance services executives were more anxious than ever to do the deal; however, Borelli resisted that one as well. He thought it could be what he termed a "huge disaster" because Marsh and McLennan could not protect itself against contingent liabilities. By that point, the insurance services executives "were really upset with me, to say the least," Borelli says.

In March of 1997, a fourth opportunity presented itself; this time, the target was a top-rate competitor, Johnson and Higgins. That acquisition met Borelli's three criteria and created substantial value for the company. By resisting the temptation to do unattractive deals even when a major competitor was also considering them, Marsh and McLennan left itself in a good position to take advantage of a better opportunity when it came along. Borelli believes that if Marsh and McLennan had acquired the much less attractive Alexander and Alexander, it would not have been in a position to acquire Johnson and Higgins. "You can only digest so much," he says.

Another example of discipline in the pricing process comes from Saint-Gobain, the French manufacturing and distribution company. Every acquisition is expected to improve its prior year's return on equity in the first year after being acquired and exceed its pre-acquisition return on assets by the third year. CFO Jean-François Phelizon explains that Saint-Gobain takes a global approach to analyzing its acquisitions; "We compare the value created by the acquisition to the value that could be created by buying back our own shares." If the later generates more value, the acquisition is not made.

Some companies routinely review each completed acquisition rigorously to better understand what makes for success or failure. That, too, is a form of process discipline. Other companies keep data on the performance of previous acquisitions to help them price future deals. Nearly all the companies in our study used some kind of a post-transaction monitoring process to track how well the acquisition or merger was performing relative to expectations and to draw lessons about what should be done differently in the future.

The lessons on pricing acquisitions and mergers that we have outlined here are straightforward. In fact, they may strike readers of this book as simple common sense. We would not disagree with that judgment. Yet the fact remains that over half the deals being done today will destroy value for the acquiring company's shareholders.

What is the reason for the disparity between these simple lessons and these poor results? We believe that far too many companies neglect the organizational discipline needed to ensure that analytical rigor triumphs over emotion and ego. Such discipline is the responsibility of executive managers and the board of directors. If the returns to shareholders from acquisitions and mergers over the next ten years are no better than they have been for the past 100, it will be because companies have not created systematic corporate governance processes that put these simple lessons into practice.

Chapter 17: What You Can't Afford to Ignore

You have a high-performing organization, a high-performing leadership team and your company culture is solid. You have come a long way from the early days. Your business has grown from a small startup to a business that other companies want to buy. Now what?

Mergers and acquisitions can fail for a variety of reasons, but what you can't afford to ignore are poor culture fit and human capital issues.

Your human resources team plays a key role in preparing for and getting you and your employees through a merger or acquisition. From cultural integration and effective communication to change management, don't forget the human side of the merger.

There are things that you can do to help prevent your company from becoming a mergers and acquisitions statistic.

Determine whether it's a good cultural fit.

Many times a company is attractive as an acquisition target because of its company culture. Successful mergers often are ones where the companies' cultures and values are similar.

While every business will have its own company culture, this is one area that will make a difference if you can get a close match to your acquiring company and if it's not a match, is one company or the other willing to change to make things better?

When a merger or acquisition is imminent, your employees may be asked to tell the buyer what it's like to work at your company. There may be surveys, leadership interviews or focus groups. This is all part of the preparation process to determine whether the cultures are a good fit.

Culture alignment isn't a step you can afford to ignore in the merger process. Remember, many mergers fail because what looks great on paper, may not always add up if the two cultures simply aren't compatible. You don't want to get down the road and have to pull the plug at the last minute because you overlooked this phase.

Build a communication plan.

Just as critical as planning for culture fit is the need to communicate throughout the merger process. A clear and thoughtful communication plan can go a long way in easing concerns, distrust and resistance as employees are challenged to go from the known to the unknown. Early on, sit down with your HR team and come up with a timeline of what will happen, what will be communicated, and when. Not everyone will find out at the same time and some communication will go only to certain groups.

Items you'll want to consider.

1. Who needs to know about the merger and acquisition? You will be communicating with employees, customers, channel partners, vendors, media, etc.

2. Who needs to buy into the changes resulting from the acquisition? You should have a core team of early adopters who will be your champions of change. Your leadership team should be unified in how it presents itself and information.

3. Who and what will be impacted and how? This can include anything from processes and deadlines to whether there will be job reassignments.

4. How will you communicate each piece of information? In print, email, general announcement, formal letters, press release, website or social media? It will depend on the audience and the formality of the announcement. Some communication will have to be vetted by your legal counsel to ensure the information is accurate and aligned with the merger agreement.

5. Establish a timeline. What types of milestones will you put in place? For example; by 60 days out, we will have job assignments made. By 30 days all employees will have met with their supervisor.

Having a communication plan and timeline provides vision and clarity to your leadership and assures your employees that you are attentive to how this affects them.

Focus on change management.

One of the biggest reasons mergers and acquisitions fail is due to poor change management. As a result, how you interact with employees and manage the change process can be the difference between success and failure as you merge two organizations. This is where your communication plan and leadership team alignment will pay off.

As you get closer to transitioning, there are workforce issues that will need to be addressed. The timing of these will have been established in the communication plan. There is no set formula for the timeline, as each merger or acquisition has its own needs.

1. What will the organization chart of the combined organizations look like? Determine job titles and the reporting hierarchy.

2. Do you have the right people in the right jobs? Which managers will you need and in what key roles?

3. Do you need to reorganize? Is there overlap on positions? Some organizations will have their people interview for their jobs to ensure there is alignment moving forward.

4. Review the compensation philosophy of each company. If you will use the benefits and payroll

systems of the acquiring company, you need to communicate that to your employees.

5. What is the performance evaluation and reward system? Do you need to do a skills inventory or audit of your current staff?

6. Your employees should learn about the new company; its history, its culture and its processes. This could range from a cultural immersion program to a welcome breakfast sponsored by the acquiring company.

7. Share the handbook of the new company with your employees and highlight items that may be different from how you typically do things.

You may find that you stumble along the way and that is bound to happen. But, in dealing with human resources issues, take note of these potential oversights
   a. Not involving an HR professional early on.
   b. Not thoroughly understanding employee needs and concerns.
   c. Not engaging and guiding the leadership team.
   d. Not carving out enough time and resources for a successful integration.

Leadership doesn't happen in a vacuum.

At the end of the day, the success or failure of this endeavour may rest heavily on your leadership style and company culture.

While you may be focused on the financial and legal details surrounding a merger or acquisition, remember that you will need a strong human capital guidance system. Be as prepared as you can be with a communication plan, timeline and transition plan that keeps your workforce in mind; because this takes a lot of work and there are pitfalls that you want to avoid, you may want to outsource all or part of the human resources effort. You could choose to have a company take over the day-to-day HR administration such as payroll and benefits administration or ask third party company to help you develop a strategic plan to get you through the merger.

Having your i's dotted and t's crossed before you get to a merger or acquisition can go a long way in determining whether the deal is successful.

Chapter 18: Acquisition Mistakes You Can't Afford to Make

On the other seller side. I have seen few acquisitions work out well. It's one of the reasons I hate to see sellers provide seller financing or have a large part of their sale based on contingencies. Buyers will often blame the seller when things don't go well. It then becomes easy for your buyer to stop paying the note…..Then what do you do?

It's all about culture.

When I did my first acquisitions; I never even knew what the term corporate culture meant. I never realized that other companies would do things differently than we did.

When I bought my first business our company did things one way and the company we bought which did things very differently. I thought that logically they would of course adopt our way of doing things. Boy, was I wrong. What happened was a minor disaster. It took me several years to get the people at the company we bought to adopt our method of doing things.

At the end of the day, the buyer will always control what the culture will be. If the culture isn't compatible, the chance of a successful acquisition drops; the amount depends on how skilful you as the acquiring company is at merging multiple cultures.

Buyers are more optimistic than they should be.

This was certainly true for me. When we bought our first businesses we thought that tons of expenses would disappear. That never happened. In fact, most of the time when we did an acquisition, during the first year or two expenses would go up. We spent a lot of time and money getting the businesses we bought up to our standards.

If you are about to buy a business understand that there will always be things you didn't expect. If you don't budget for the unexpected you just might find yourself short of cash. It happened to me and it could very easily happen to you.

Then there is behavioural finance.

I call this my restaurant story. I was in the food business and decided we should keep our catering staff busy by opening a restaurant. We found a spot and I just kept negotiating with the landlord and before I knew it I had put so much effort into making the deal work that I wasn't about to back out. I rationally knew there was no way this was going to end well and yet I kept negotiating.

As you might expect, it didn't end well. After leaving my $50,000 deposit I ended my adventure in owning a restaurant. This can even be worse when you go to buy someone else's business. You have to have a trigger for when you are going to walk away. You need to have someone who is going to remind you when the trigger has been hit. Then, you have to listen. If you don't you are going to fall prey to what is called sunk costs; that is when you have put in so much effort, you just don't want to walk away.

Watch out for your ego.

I recently was involved with a client where one of the leaders of the company decided that acquisitions were the way to grow. No one else at the firm was interested in pursuing this strategy. He kept at it and wouldn't back down. Eventually, he had to leave the firm because he lost all support from other key leaders.

Let's face it; buying a business is good for your ego. It's fun to buy a business. Too often I see a bidding war start between two buyers. All the players decide they "need" to own the company they are after. They let their ego get in the way and before you know it, they have bought a business where they have paid way too much money. Don't let this happen to you.

The deal structure.

By deal structure I mean the real cost of the deal. You see if you pay someone $1,000,000 for their business you are going to end up paying them more than that. If you buy stock the price will likely be closer to $1,800,000. That is because you have to earn enough to pay taxes before you actually pay for the business.

Even if you do an asset sale you are likely going to have a tax cost that you don't recapture for years. This is especially true with goodwill. Even though you

127

get to deduct goodwill, you have to take fifteen years to do so. You have already either paid the seller or the bank back using after tax dollars before you get your deduction.

This is when owner financing becomes especially dangerous. Too often I have seen sellers not factor whether the buyer can afford to pay them. Too often the seller decides to provide owner financing. You know what happens when cash is tight; the buyer will just stop paying you and, I bet you don't want that to happen.

All is not lost.

Here is the deal. Acquisitions can work. You need to think about problems you will have. You have to learn to say no. You have to learn to walk away from the deal when it's not in your favour. You need to have a thinking partner who is going to help you in this process. If not, you will end up with my early acquisition results and this is not something I want you to achieve; it's just too painful.

Chapter 19: The Best Leveraged Buyout To-date.

Is the Blackstone's $26 Billion Hilton Deal.

In the early spring of 2009, with the recession deepening, Christopher Nassetta stood alone in an empty house in Arlington, Va., surrounded by moving boxes and trying not to despair. What he hoped would be the crowning achievement of his career-executing, as chief executive officer, the turnaround of Hilton Worldwide Holdings (HLT), the legendary hotel company founded by Paris Hilton's great-grandfather had turned nightmarish. He did just returned to the East Coast after closing Hilton's Beverly Hills headquarters, and that was the least of his troubles.

Eighteen months earlier, in the fall of 2007, Blackstone Group (BX) had bought Hilton in a $26 billion leveraged buyout at the height of the real estate bubble. Jonathan Gray, Blackstone's global head of real estate and the architect of the Hilton deal, invested $5.6 billion of Blackstone's money and had big plans for revitalizing the chain, the epitome of cosmopolitan glamour in the Mad Men era. Central to Gray's plans had been hiring Nassetta away from Host Hotels & Resorts (HST), where he was CEO.

At Hilton, the two got off to a decent enough start, but then, as the financial crisis hit and the economy tanked, it appeared that Blackstone and its partners had paid too much, used too much debt, and couldn't have picked a worse moment to close the deal. Some of its partners among them, Bear Stearns and Lehman Brothers would soon cease to exist. After Lehman's collapse, tourism went into a severe slump, Hilton slumped, too, and it appeared that all of Nassetta's bright ideas for restoring the chain's lustre would never get implemented. Adding insult to injury, rival Starwood Hotels & Resorts Worldwide (HOT) sued Hilton in federal court, alleging that Hilton employees had stolen the plans for its successful W Hotel franchises in what it called "the clearest imaginable case of corporate espionage, theft of trade secrets, unfair competition, and computer fraud." The Department of Justice began investigating Starwood's charges.

"Revenue's running down 20 percent," Gray recalls. "Cash flow is down around 30 percent. We get a huge suit. The Department of Justice opens up an investigation. It was definitely a low moment in the deal." Blackstone was in serious danger of losing the bulk of its $5.6 billion. "I promise you this is the absolute bottom," Nassetta recalls Gray telling him that summer, bucking himself up, too. "How can it get any worse than this?"

Four years later, when Blackstone took the company public in December 2013, its timing proved impeccable and in July 2014, when Hilton's stock closed at $24.80, Gray and Nassetta had officially transformed Hilton into the most lucrative private equity deal ever, with a paper profit of $12 billion.

One key to this good fortune is obvious; the historically low interest rates maintained by the Federal Reserve. But plenty of other deals benefited from low lending rates, too, and fell apart. In fact, one of the nine hospitality and lodging LBOs completed in the same time frame as Blackstone's Hilton acquisition, only Hilton and La Quinta Inns and Suites (another Blackstone deal) were not forced into bankruptcy or a debt restructuring.

The full story of the richest LBO in history is actually a story of private equity working as advertised. By persuading its lenders to exercise forbearance, restructuring its debt before it had to, and practicing smart management, as opposed to indiscriminate cost cuts and pink slips, Blackstone made Hilton perform better than most thought possible.

"There weren't many people in the room with me who still believed," Gray says of 2009. "But the good news is we were able to say, 'Look, we have got plenty of cash'. I don't think we ever went below a billion dollars in cash on our balance sheet and, 'We really believe in this business.'" Still, he confides, he had to filter out the negativity while he waited for things to improve. "It's no fun reading that you are not very smart."

While he is familiar to some investment bankers because of Blackstone's history of savvy real estate deals, especially the purchase of Equity Office Properties Trust, Gray, 44, is little known outside Wall Street. A billionaire (his Blackstone shares are valued at about $1.3 billion), he's a Phi Beta Kappa graduate of the University of Pennsylvania and determinedly low-key "annoyingly calm," his wife, Mindy, says. He prefers philanthropy to a Hamptons manse, spending time with Mindy and their four daughters over parties and auctions. He does own a five-bedroom apartment on Park Avenue but drives a Toyota minivan and wears a plastic Timex watch!

Chapter 20: Turning Around Underperforming Businesses.

With business conditions set to remain challenging for most industries from time to time, it's worth taking time to review best-practice turnaround techniques to ensure you and your management team not only protect your business, but also use this period as an opportunity to strengthen your market position.

The following points should be top of mind when developing and executing a turnaround or transformation strategy.

1. Stakeholder Management is Key.

While it's important to focus significant attention on financial and operational restructuring; any business that places sole attention here and ignores stakeholder management will suffer the consequences. Good stakeholder management involves communicating with all key parties; financiers, employees, shareholders, unions, creditors and customers. Turning a business around is as much about maintaining confidence as it is to implementing the right initiatives. Most turnarounds fail due to insufficient focus on stakeholder management; particularly employee engagement.

2. One to Two Big Changes in Strategy.

Nine times out of 10 you need to develop one or two big changes in your business strategy. Very rarely is there a quick fix or simply some fine tuning required.

Maintaining stakeholder support is crucial and being able to demonstrate "what will be different going forward" is the key. Simply relying on external factors to improve won't cut it. You need to demonstrate that not only will the one or two big changes in strategy help protect your business from external shocks but they will materially change your earnings outlook.

Here are some examples of the types of big changes we are referring to.

1. Rationalising your product or service offering back to your core more profitable products (often a reduction of 25-30%). This will typically require some redundancies to right-size the cost base.
2. Transforming your strategy around customer service and employee engagement.
3. Developing an online and social media strategy.
4. Selling or exiting non-core divisions or regions.
5. Developing strategic partnerships.
6. Focusing on Research and Development to develop a breakthrough product.
7. Outsourcing your manufacturing or purchasing to lower cost regions/countries.
8. Executing an acquisition or merger to generate greater economies of scale.

9. Raising equity to fund a growth strategy.

3. Relentless Execution.

Most transformation or turnaround projects fail for two reasons. Firstly, not developing the big changes required in strategy, and secondly; failing to execute the plan effectively. Restructuring plans require enormous effort and this is often too much for the existing team to manage due to existing commitments of running the business, as well as the need for specific expertise on a range of matters. That is why a Chief Restructuring Officer (CRO) is often required to project manage the restructuring plan alongside the management team. Their role is to ensure the plan is being executed accordingly, that each person responsible for their part is being held accountable and that there are no surprises. The CRO works closely with the CEO and together they drive the reform projects.

With these key principles in mind the following 5 key phases of a turnaround is a typical process to follow.

1. Analyse the situation by conducting a strategic review to determine how the business got into the position in the first place, the key risks facing the business, the key issues and recommendations to mitigate them plus strategic options for consideration.

2. Implement a stabilisation plan, including a 100-day work-plan, aggressive stakeholder and working capital

management, and identification of 'quick wins' to develop momentum.

3. Change or bolster management, which often involves changing key personnel due to underperformance, or bolstering the management team by engaging a chief restructuring officer to project manage the many and varied initiatives. This frees up management to stay focused on the core business.

4. Restructure the business, whether by changing the business model, rebranding to drive revenue, changing the customer or product mix, selling non-core assets/divisions, or redundancies.

5. Return to normal, or sell along the way if that will drive greater value for stakeholders.

No matter what business cycle you are in, these principles and techniques will serve you well and ensure that you are taking the necessary steps to protect and enhance enterprise value.

Chapter 21: Buy, Build and Sell.

One alternative to starting a business from scratch is to buy an existing business and turn it around; a method that may help you redefine your own thoughts of what a "startup" could be.

The past few years have been very profitable for entrepreneurs with an eye for turning around existing but underperforming operations, limiting their own risk while leveraging resources that already exist in the business.

Business-for-sale transactions increased in 2014, according to a recent business brokers surveyed; they expect even more businesses to change hands next year. Nearly two-thirds (61 percent) of survey respondents said that there was an increase in business succession in 2014 and about 57 percent forecast a continued rise next year.

What are the advantages of buying into an existing operation?

A customer base and some form of existing systems that could continue to be used (or upgraded) or easily replaced with more efficient technology or ways of doing business.

When you consider the expense of a conventional launch or startup, the cost of finding customers, the expenses associated with marketing and advertising, the time required to establish your own set of systems; the idea of "buy, build and sell" can be very intriguing, especially if you are just starting out in business.

If you have ever thought about taking an underperforming business off of an owner's hands, there's a lot to consider, especially in terms of the company's current numbers.

Getting to the bottom of a company's real numbers "net-net" can be a challenge in this arena. It's one reason some entrepreneurs prefer a startup; but the more businesses you look at, the more comfortable you may be in knowing the types of questions to ask and the kinds of numbers to look for.

Also be aware some businesses simply can't or won't be good candidates for turnarounds. Those include bad-concept retail businesses in poor locations, or business-to-business companies in a low demand or crowded markets (or mature markets). They represent opportunities on which you will want to pass.

Don't worry about those deals. There are better ones around, and the best place to start is to ask the simple question; "Does this company have repeat business and how much does it have?"

Repeat business over time equals profits, and if the business is generating some type of cash flow (or even slightly negative cash flow) from repeat customers, there is a good chance the business could generate consistent cash flow and profits with a few tweaks to its current operations.

"Buy, build and sell" is the terminology we use for this chapter, but you could just "buy, build and keep" if the operations side of business is what excites you.

Either way, here are some guidelines to consider that just may change the way you are thinking about getting into business. Generally, you are looking for a business that;

1. Survives despite itself: This means the business seems to be making money. It has survived for a while, and continues to, despite poor service, shoddy presentation, bad attitudes from its owners and team or general chaos or disarray.

2. Generates cash flow, as compared to being asset intensive: Buy businesses for cash flow, and leave assets to property investing. Be wary of any business with large asset investments. You are looking for cash flow versus depreciation or being saddled with large stocks of plant and equipment.

3. Can be run with low skills: You are looking for a simple business that sells things people want to buy and are buying. Most entrepreneurs won't want an architecture firm or law practice, or any business that requires huge investments of highly technical training or skills to run it.

4. Produces inferior sales and marketing materials: Poor marketing is a good sign of potential opportunity because you easily improve marketing that you can track, test and measure. Plus, if you can target it at an existing customer base, you are more than half-way to increasing extended repeat business.

5. Can be run by a great "jockey:" This means you can easily train a manager to go in and run the systems you put in place. This is especially true in a bar (hire a great bar man or woman), restaurant (hire a great chef) or salon (hire a great hairdresser). The idea can be applied to other categories as well.

6. Has a big upside: Look at the numbers. Is it a business that can net you profits of $15,000 per month versus a business that will net you $5,000? Is it running at 25% capacity and can you get it to 75% capacity in a short period of time to sell it or run it profitably? Those are some bottom-line benchmark numbers that can give you guidance in your own opportunities.

7. Is a great deal for you. Don't fall in love with the business. Fall in love with the deal. Remember, your profit is always in the purchase price. Every day, owners look to sell for a variety of different reasons. Find a win-win scenario that benefits you both. You get a great deal, and the sellers get the relief of being out of a business they don't want to run anymore, are tired of running or simply have run out of ideas "how" to operate any better.

Change your thinking about "starting up" your new business, and you just might discover a great opportunity in your own neighbourhood that you can start to work for a fraction of what it would take to do something else.

Remember, the more you get used to looking at those "deals," the better you will be at finding the perfect deal for you; one that will pay off with a big upside more than worth your investment of time and limited resources.

Good Luck!

www.ingramcontent.com/pod-product-compliance
Lightning Source LLC
Chambersburg PA
CBHW051920170526
45168CB00001B/476